MANDALA SKETCHBOOK

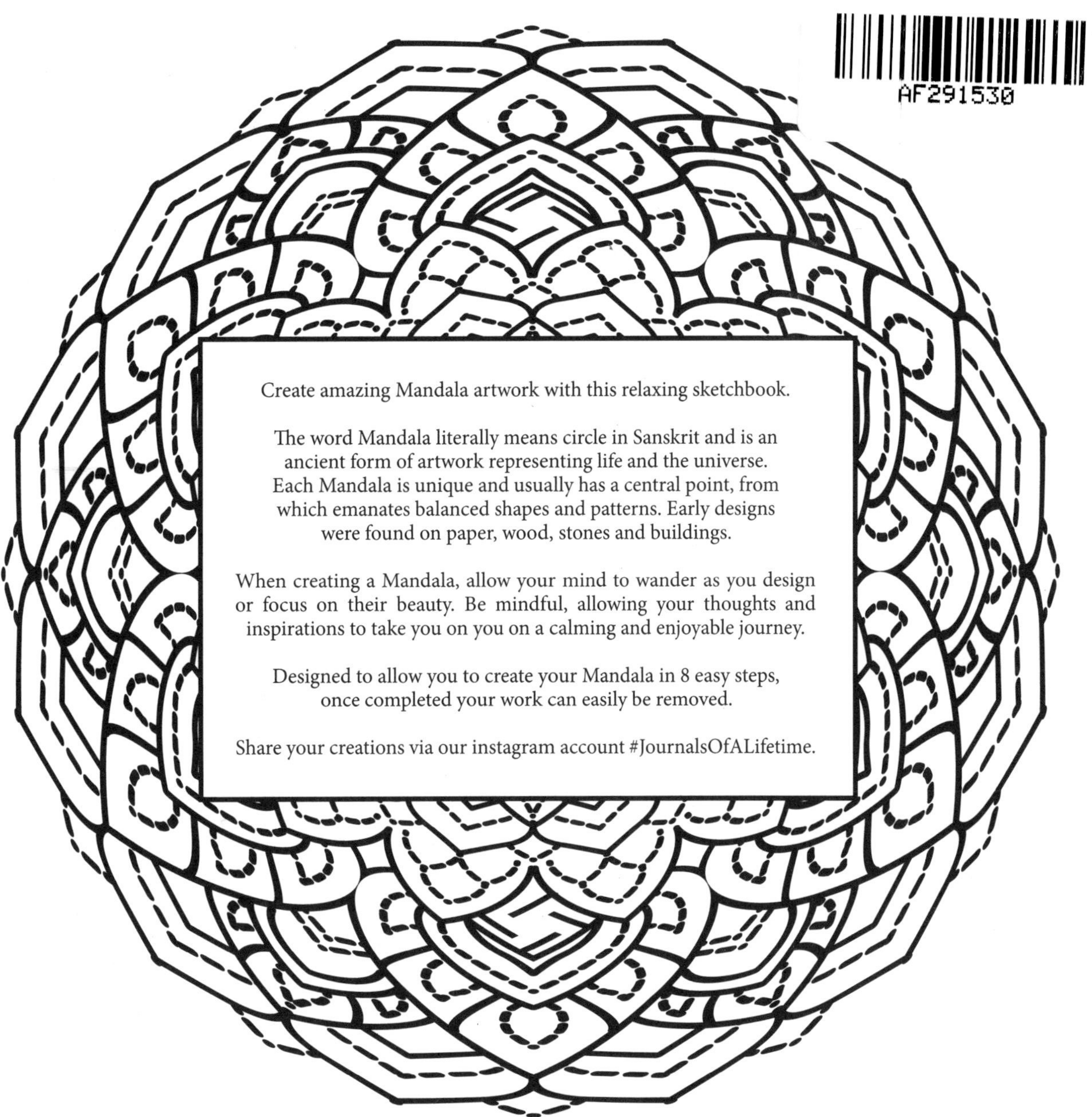

Create amazing Mandala artwork with this relaxing sketchbook.

The word Mandala literally means circle in Sanskrit and is an ancient form of artwork representing life and the universe. Each Mandala is unique and usually has a central point, from which emanates balanced shapes and patterns. Early designs were found on paper, wood, stones and buildings.

When creating a Mandala, allow your mind to wander as you design or focus on their beauty. Be mindful, allowing your thoughts and inspirations to take you on you on a calming and enjoyable journey.

Designed to allow you to create your Mandala in 8 easy steps, once completed your work can easily be removed.

Share your creations via our instagram account #JournalsOfALifetime.

MATT MANSON

HOW TO DRAW A MANDALA

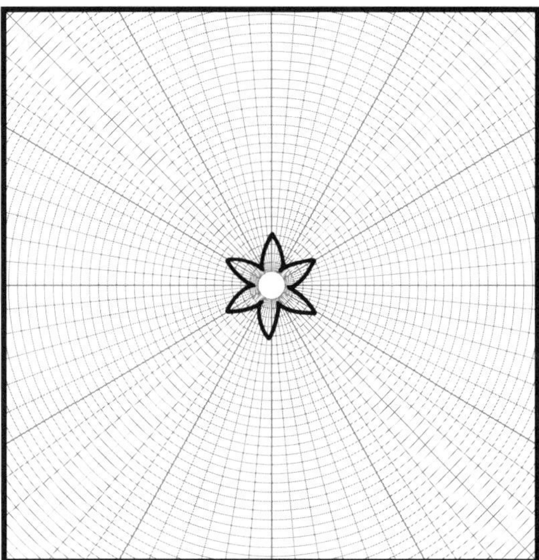

1. Think about what you would like your drawing to represent and then start by drawing a small shape in the middle of the grid.

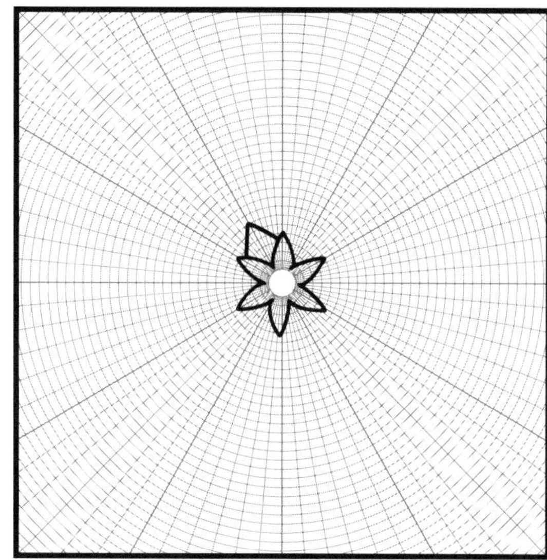

2. Now draw another shape above the first one.

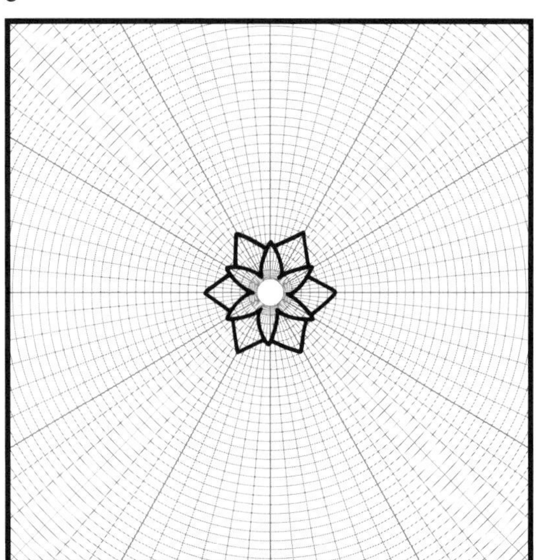

3. Using the grid system as a reference, repeat your shapes all the way around the grid to build up a symmetrical pattern.

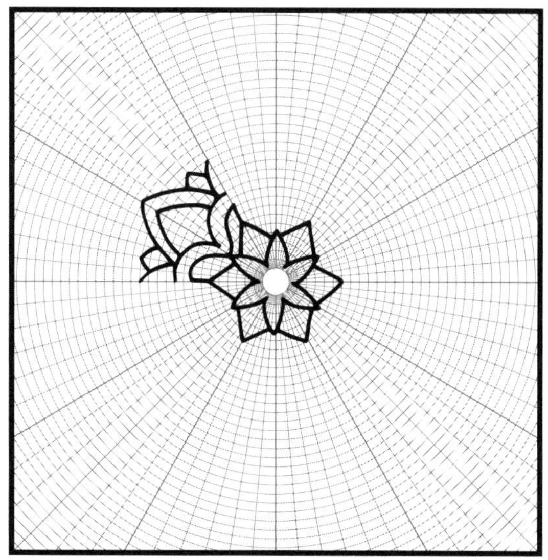

4. Keep adding new shapes above the last one, in expanding rings, working your way from the middle of the grid outwards.

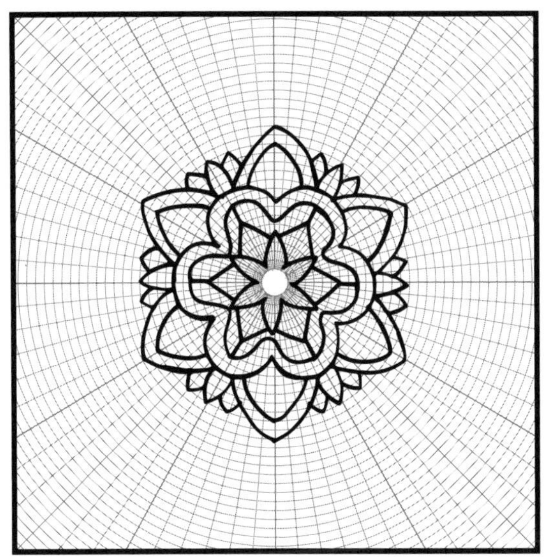

5. As you draw your next shapes keep repeating the design around the grid system.

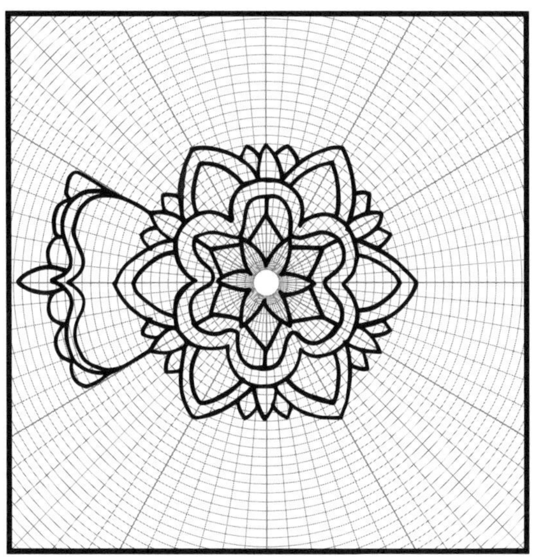

6. Work progressively outwards adding small and larger shapes and detail.

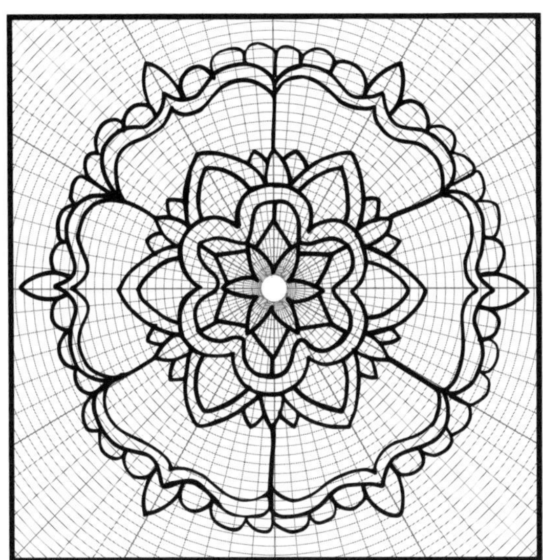

7. As your design grows you can start adding more and more intricate detail into the Mandala.

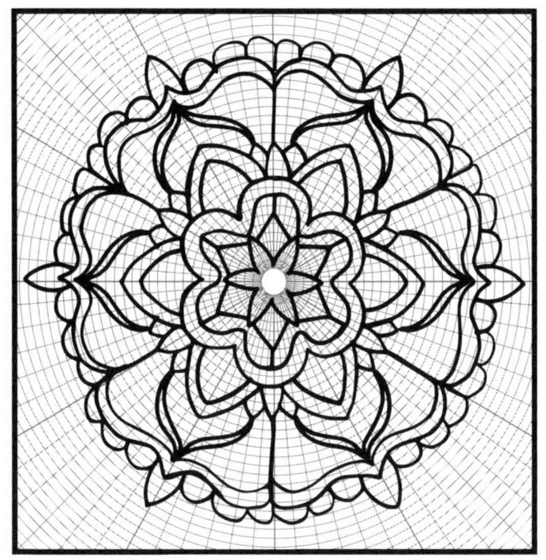

8.Fill in empty spaces with new shapes and add decoration until you have created a Mandala you are happy with.

Published by Journals Of A Lifetrime, an imprint of from you to me ltd
from you to me, The Old Brewery, Newtown, Bradford on Avon, BA15 1NF, UK

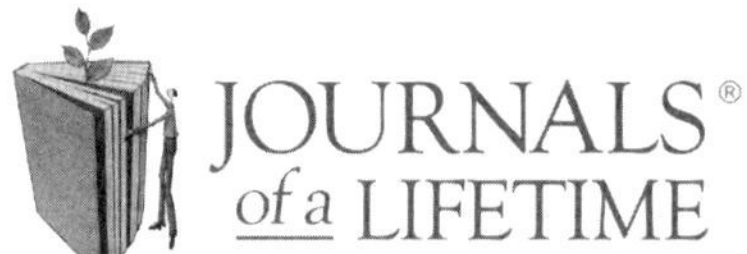

www.JournalsOfALifetime.com

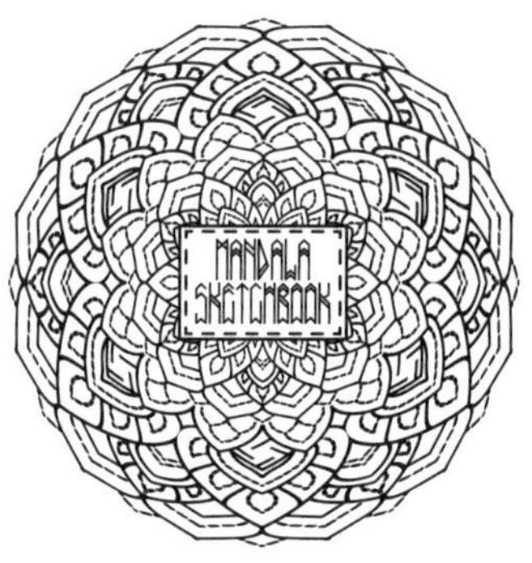

Created by Matt Manson
www.MattManson.co.uk

1 3 5 7 9 11 13 15 14 12 10 8 6 4 2

Printed and bound in China. This paper is manufactured from pulp
sourced from forests that are legally and sustainably managed.

ISBN 978-1-907860-29-4

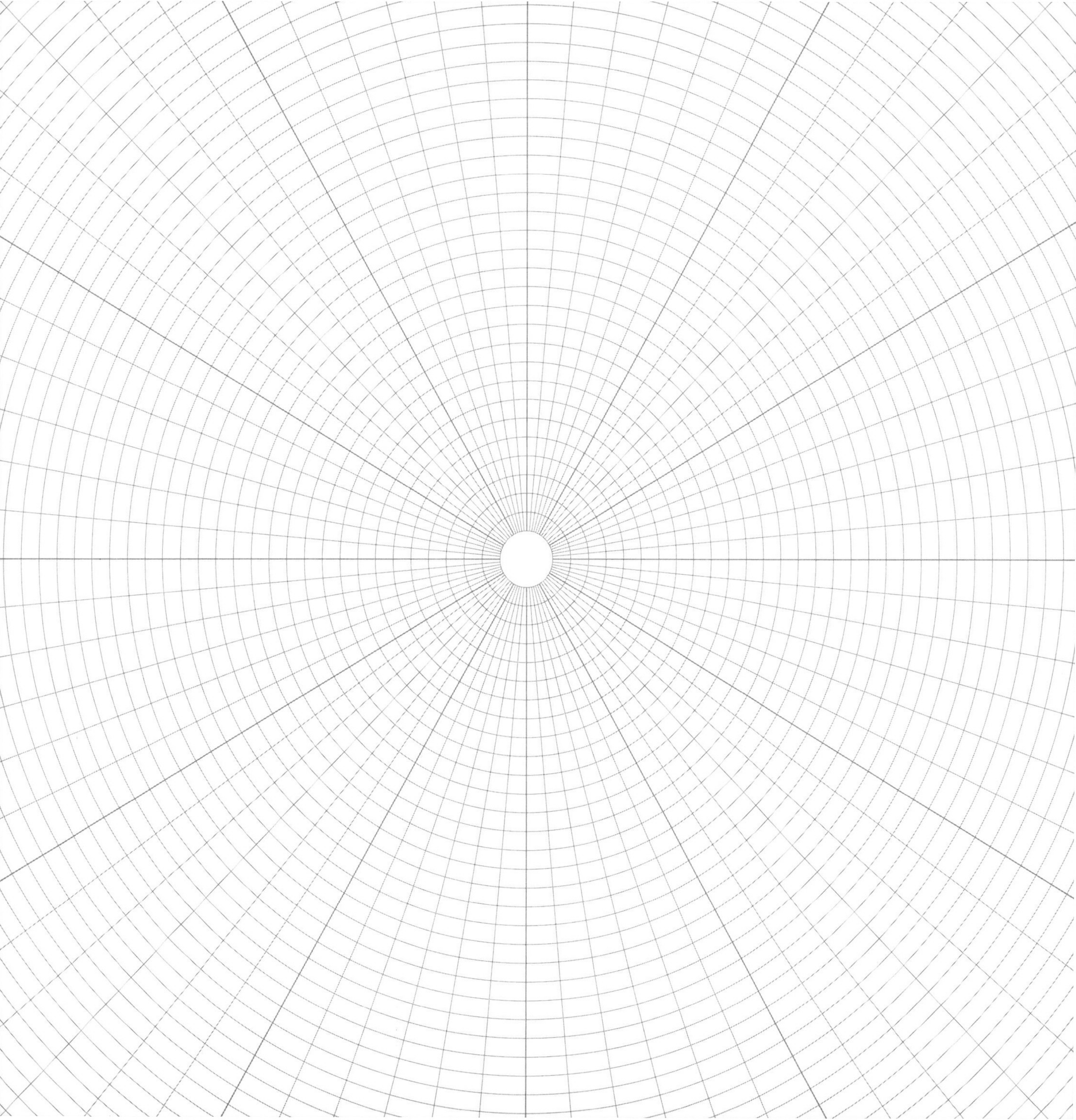

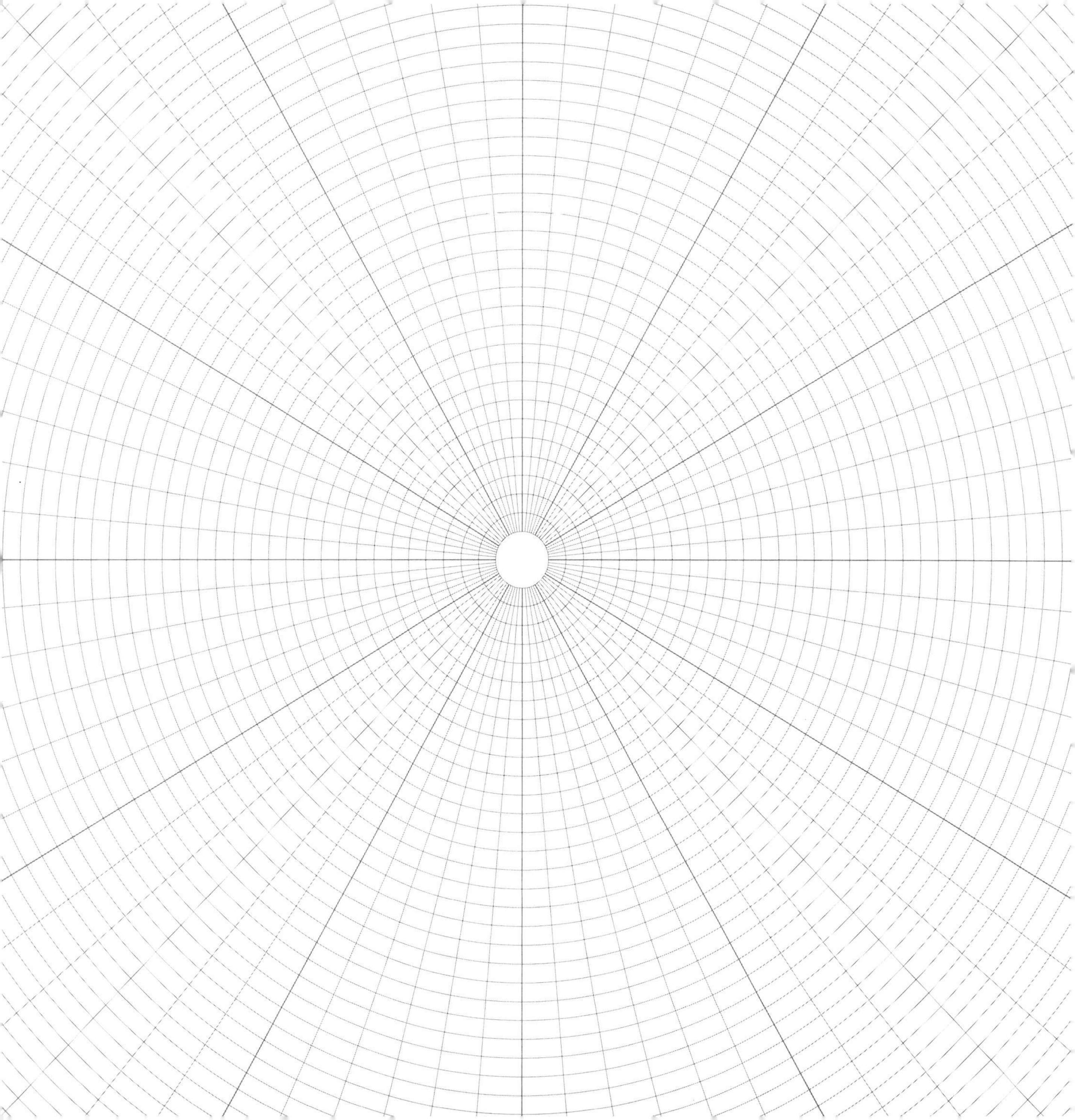

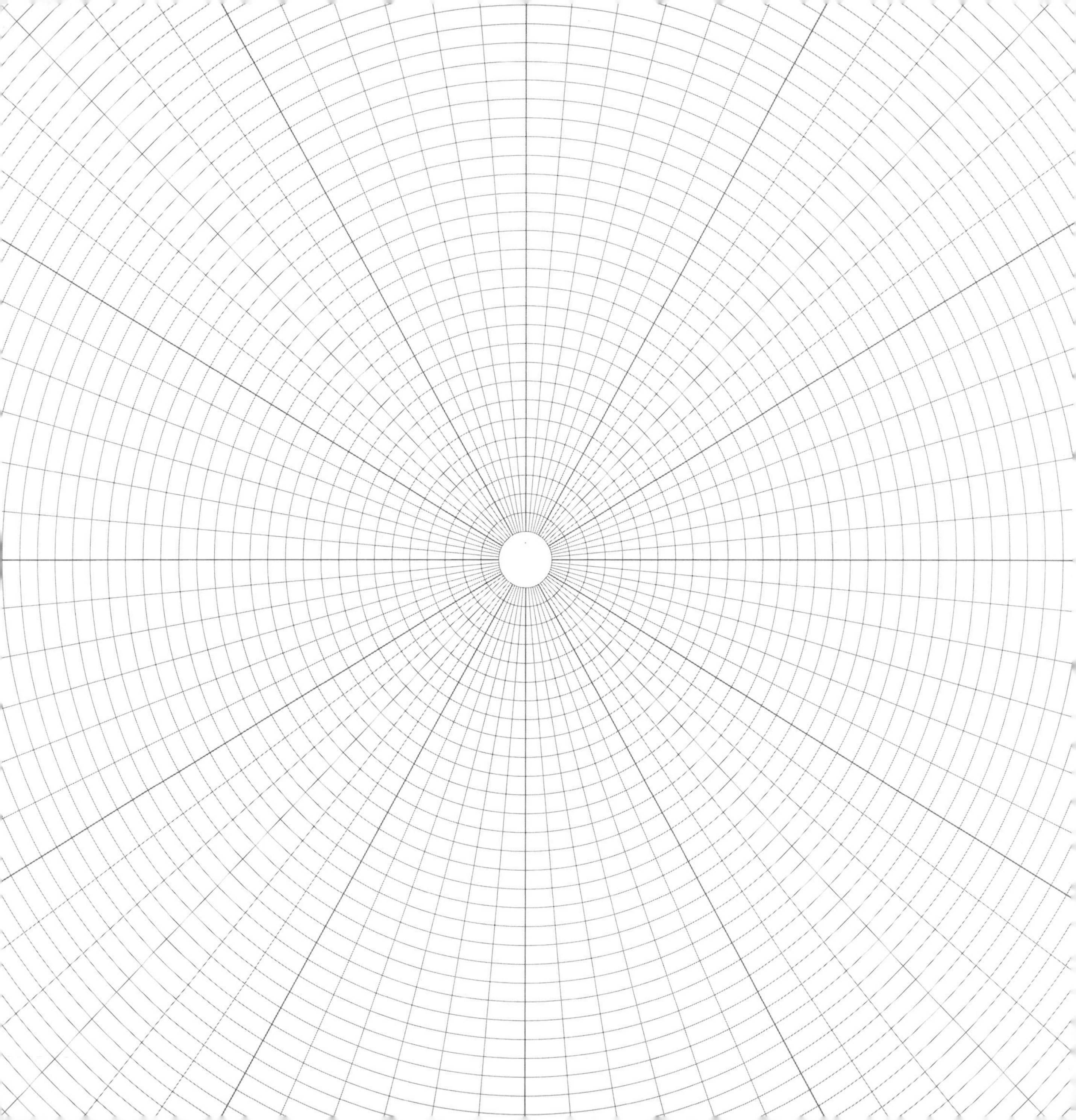

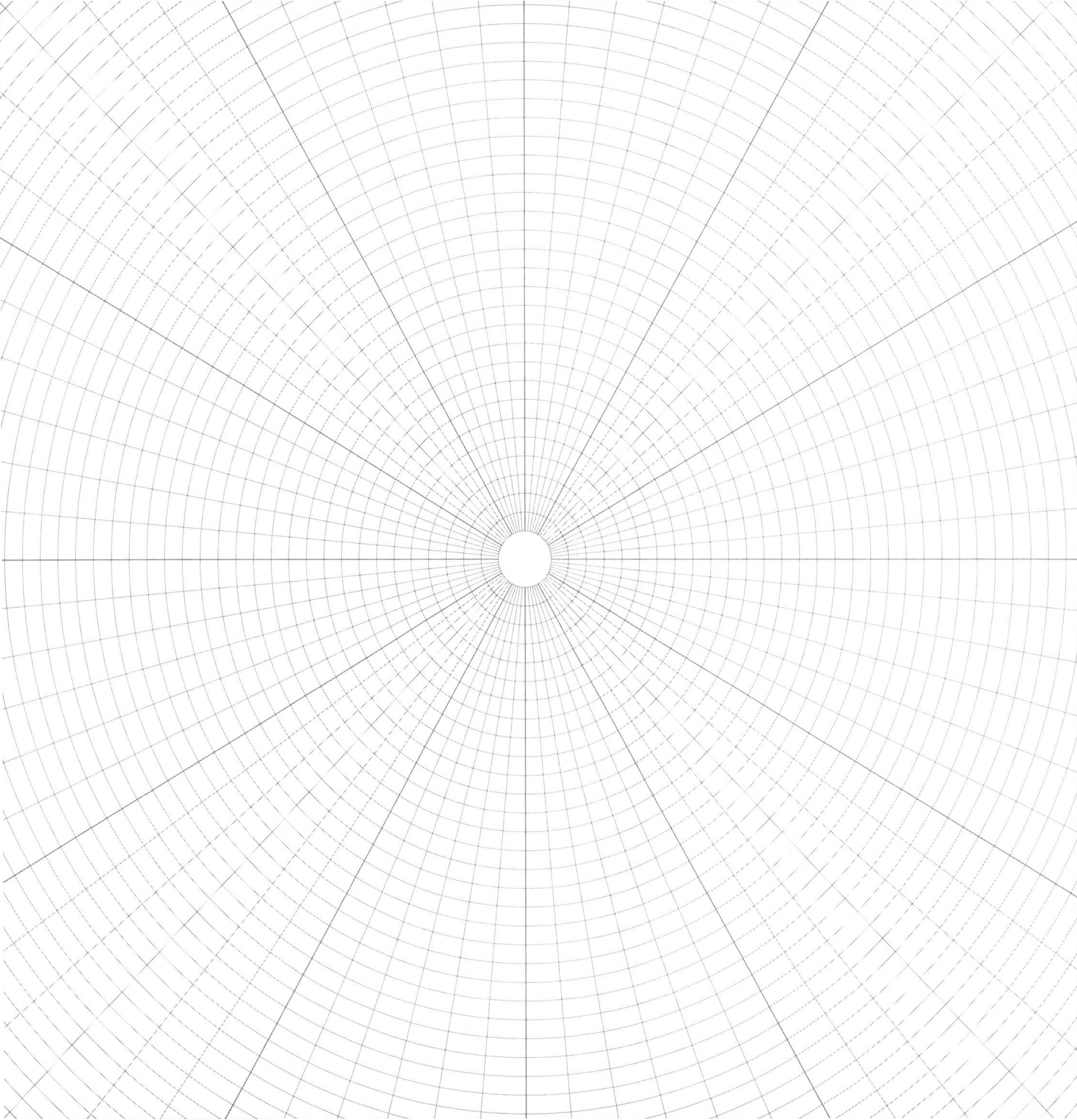

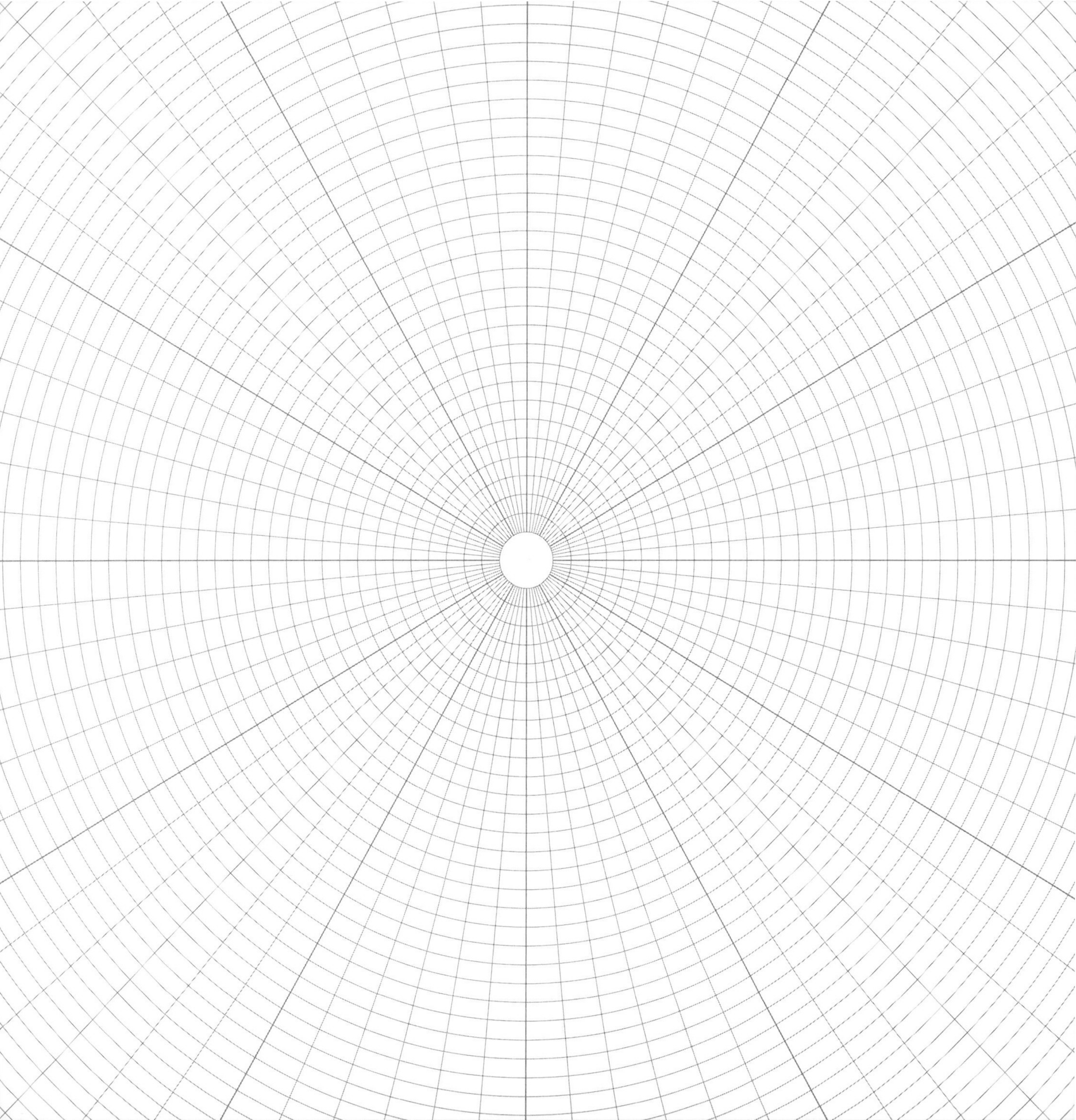

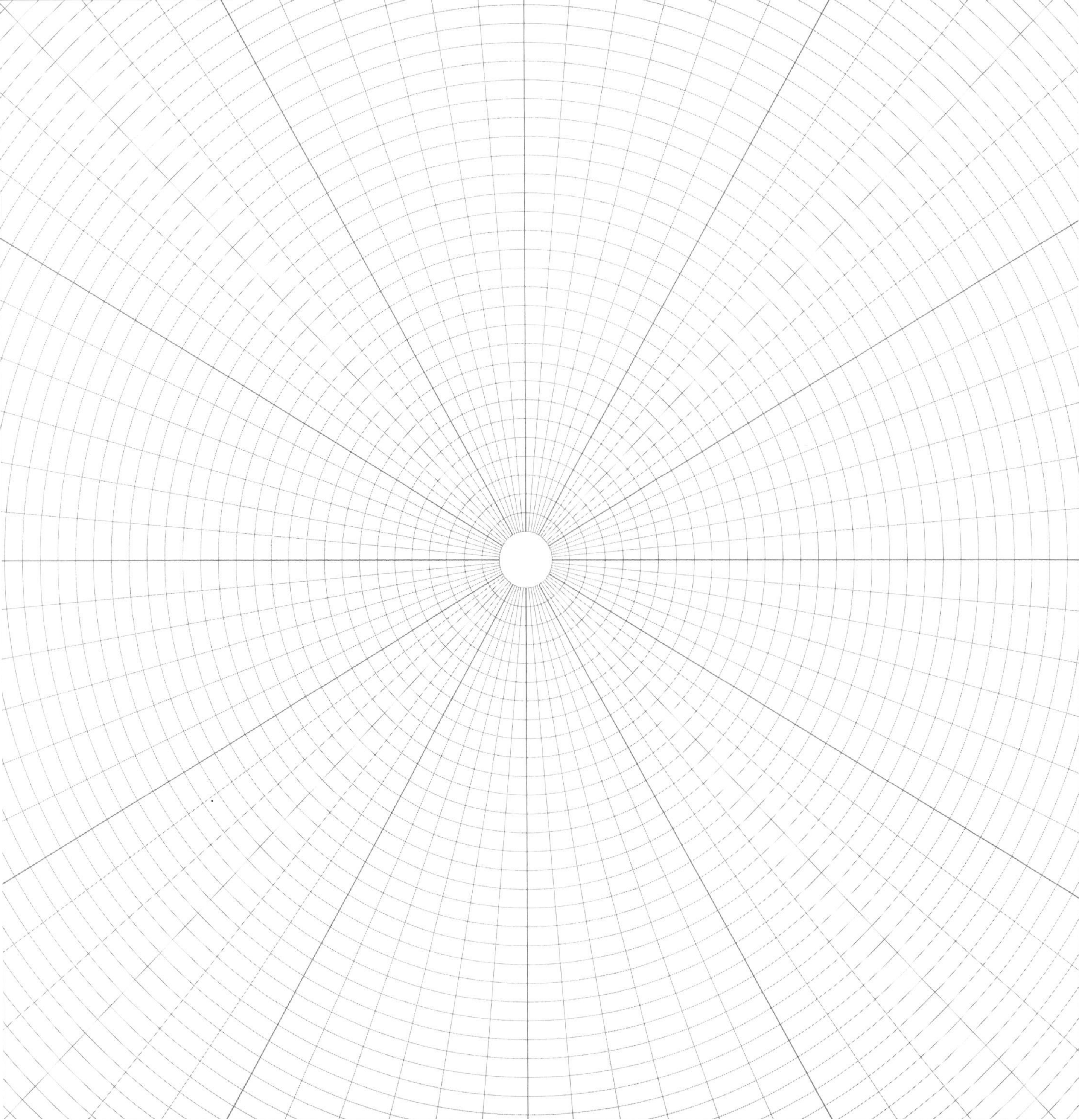

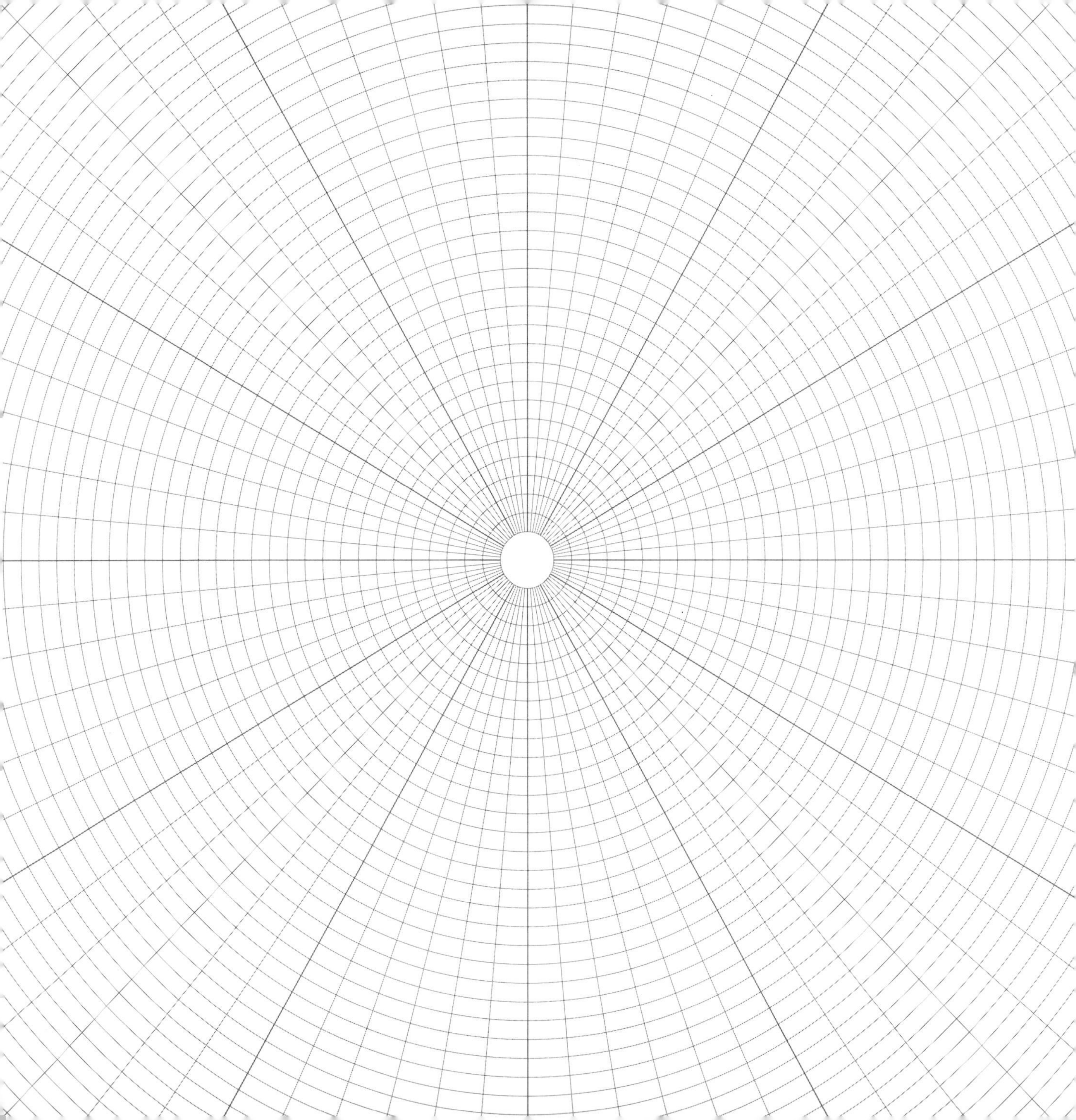

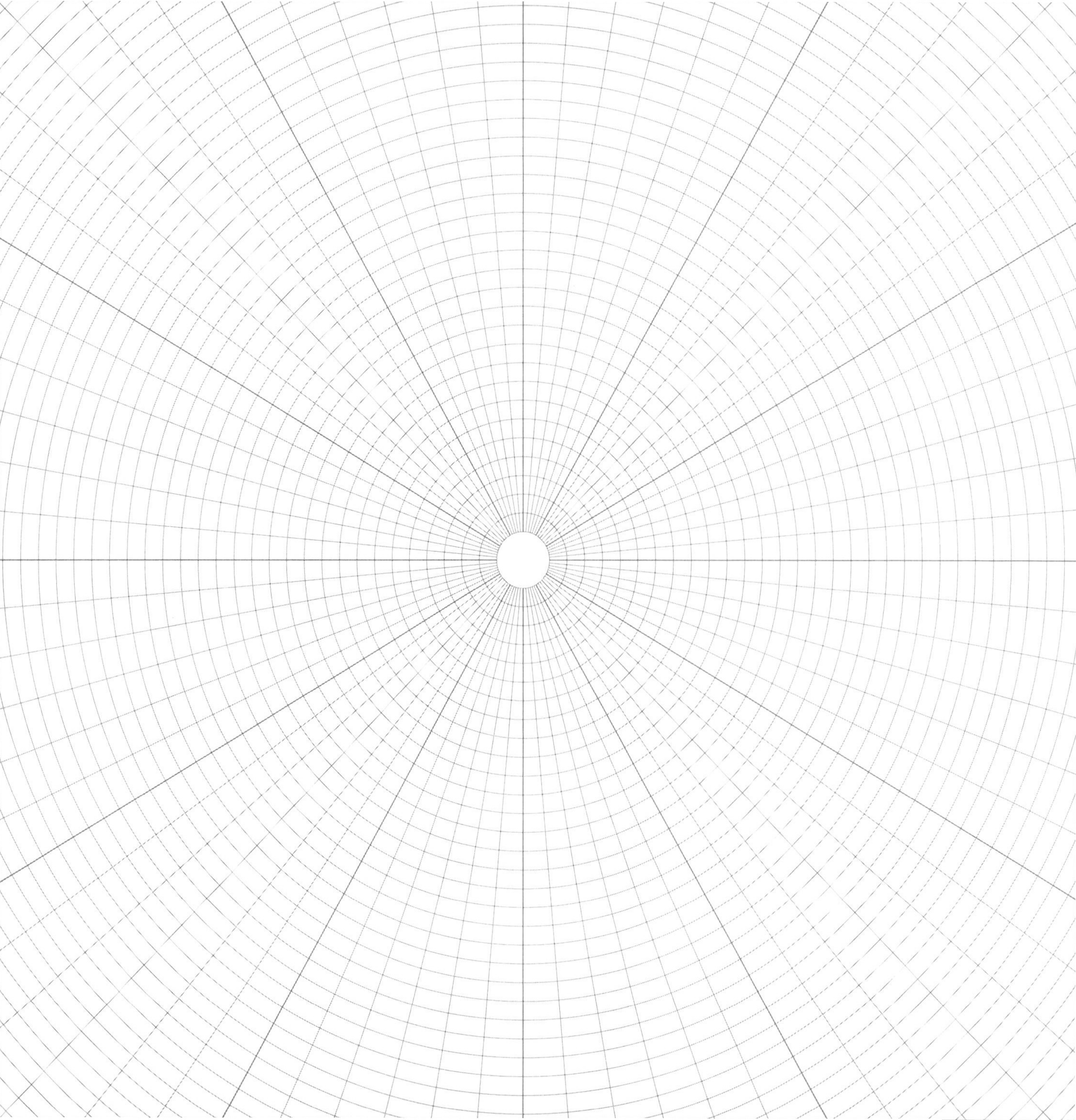

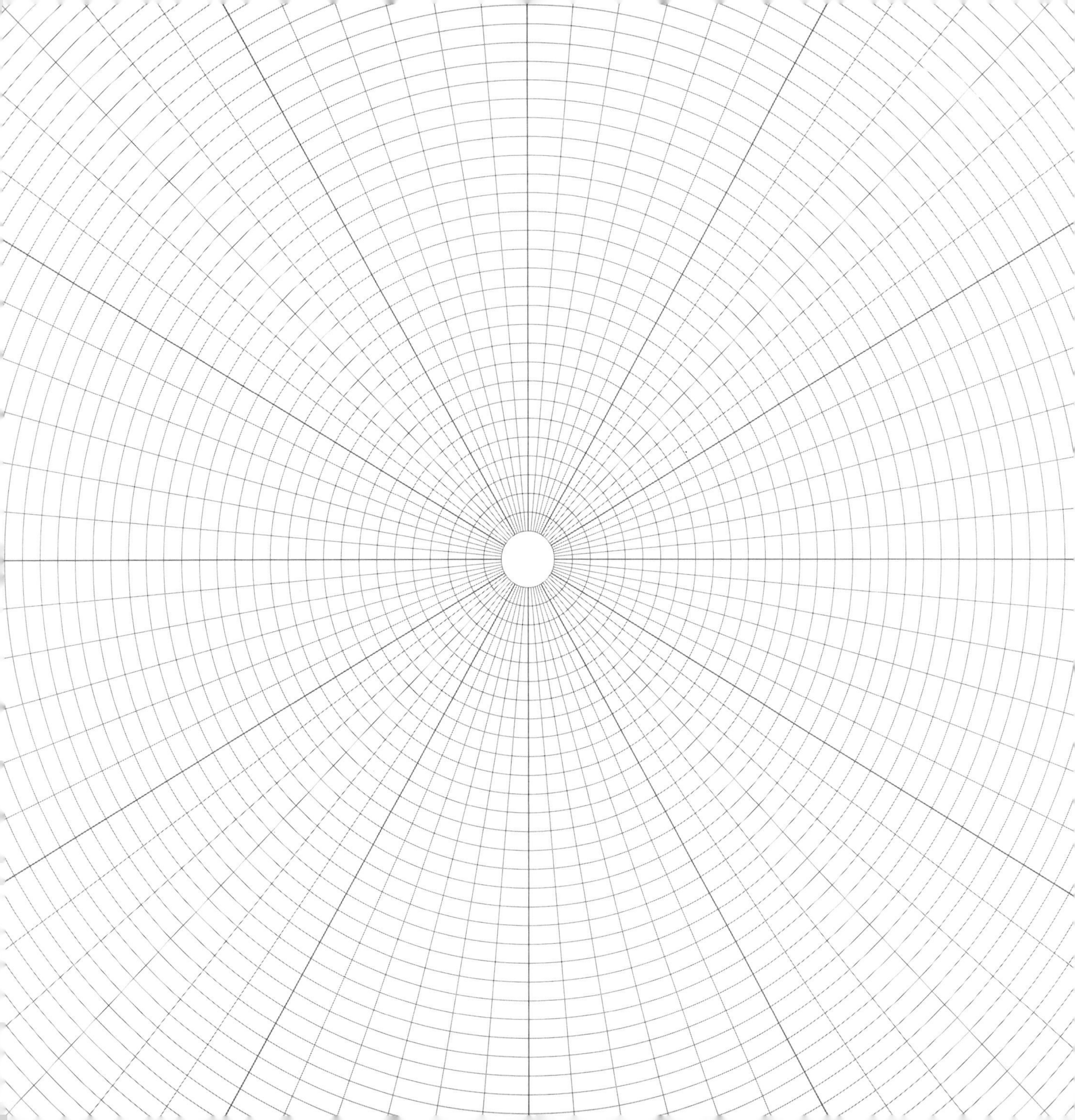

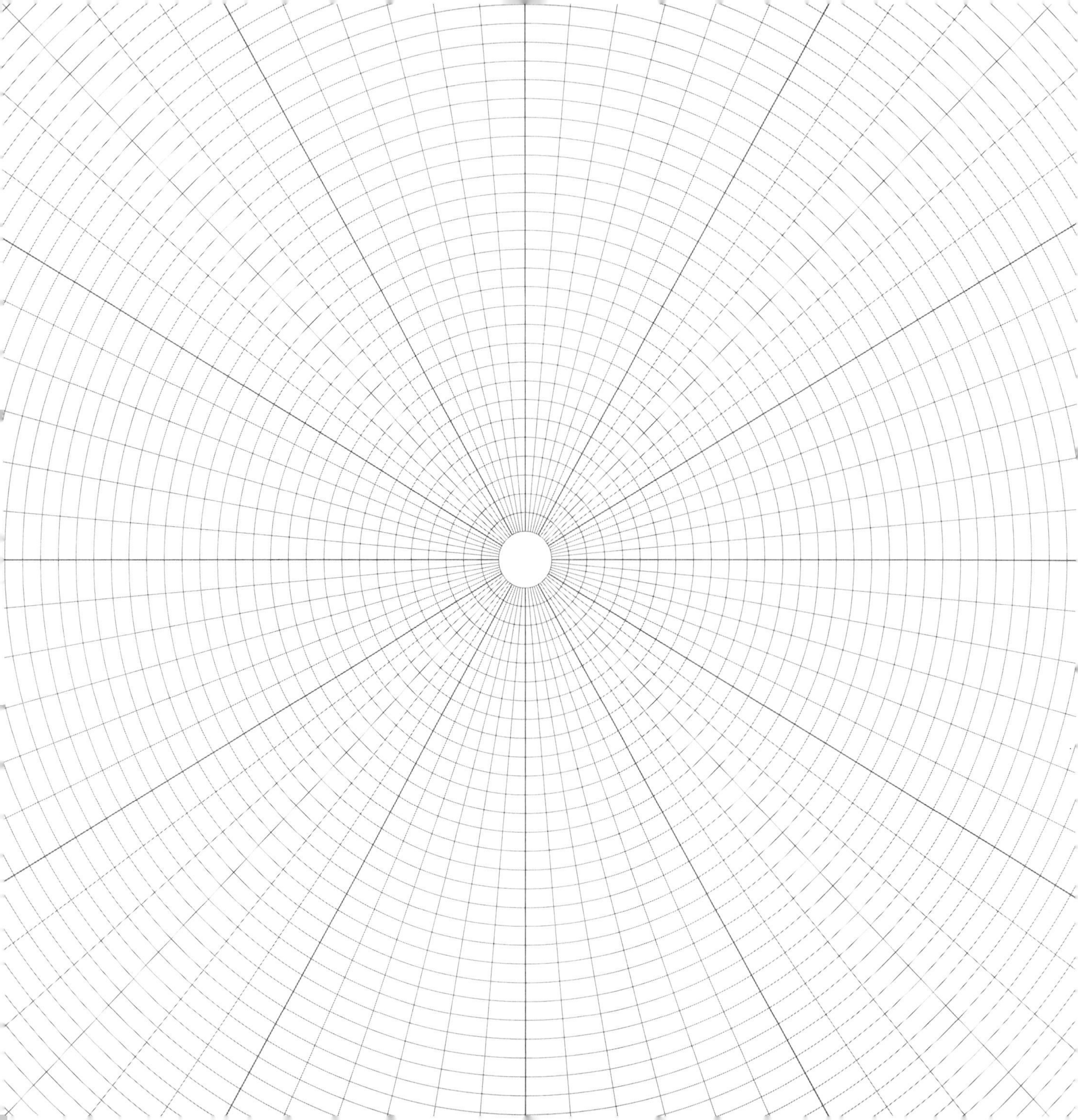

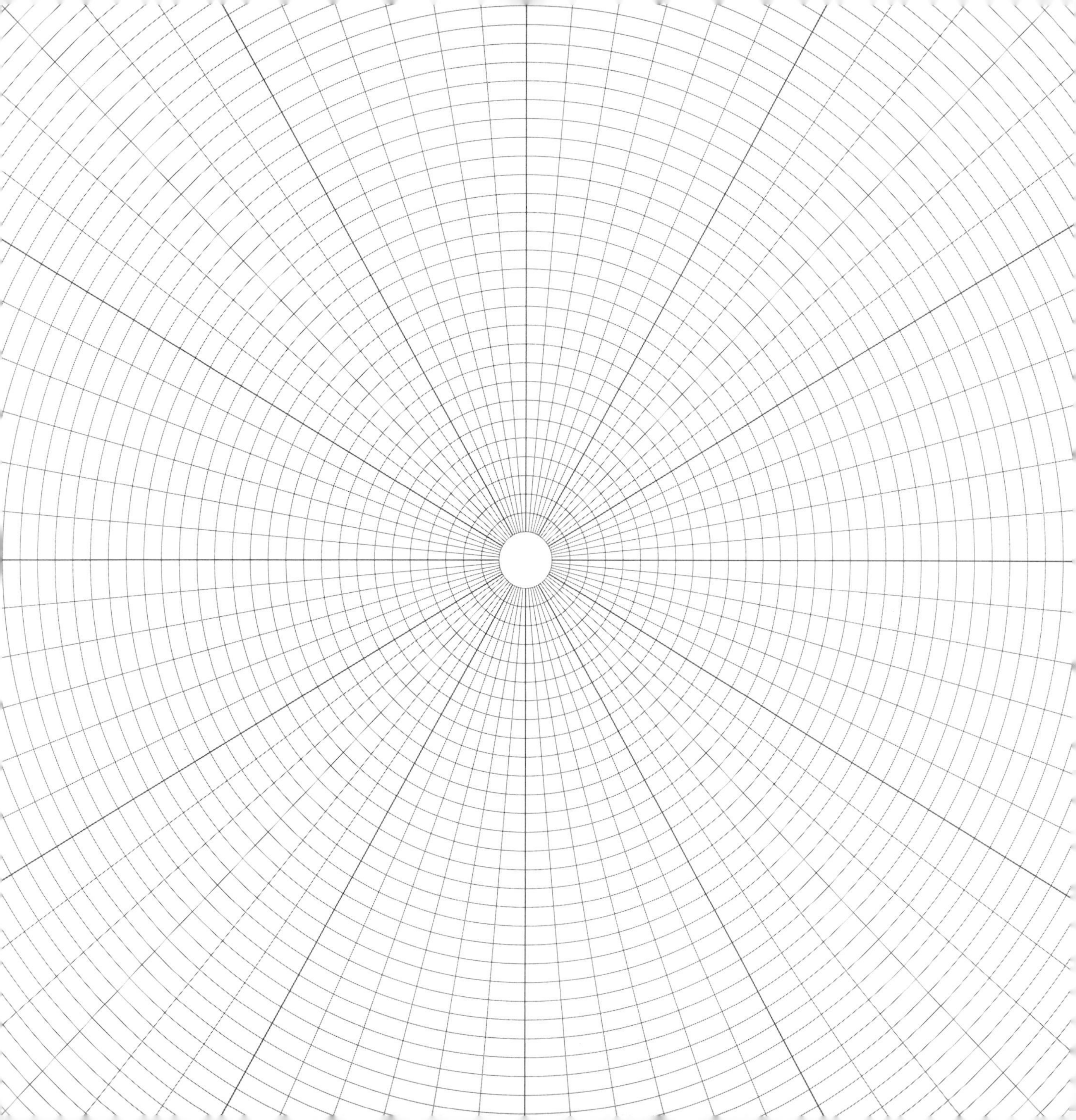

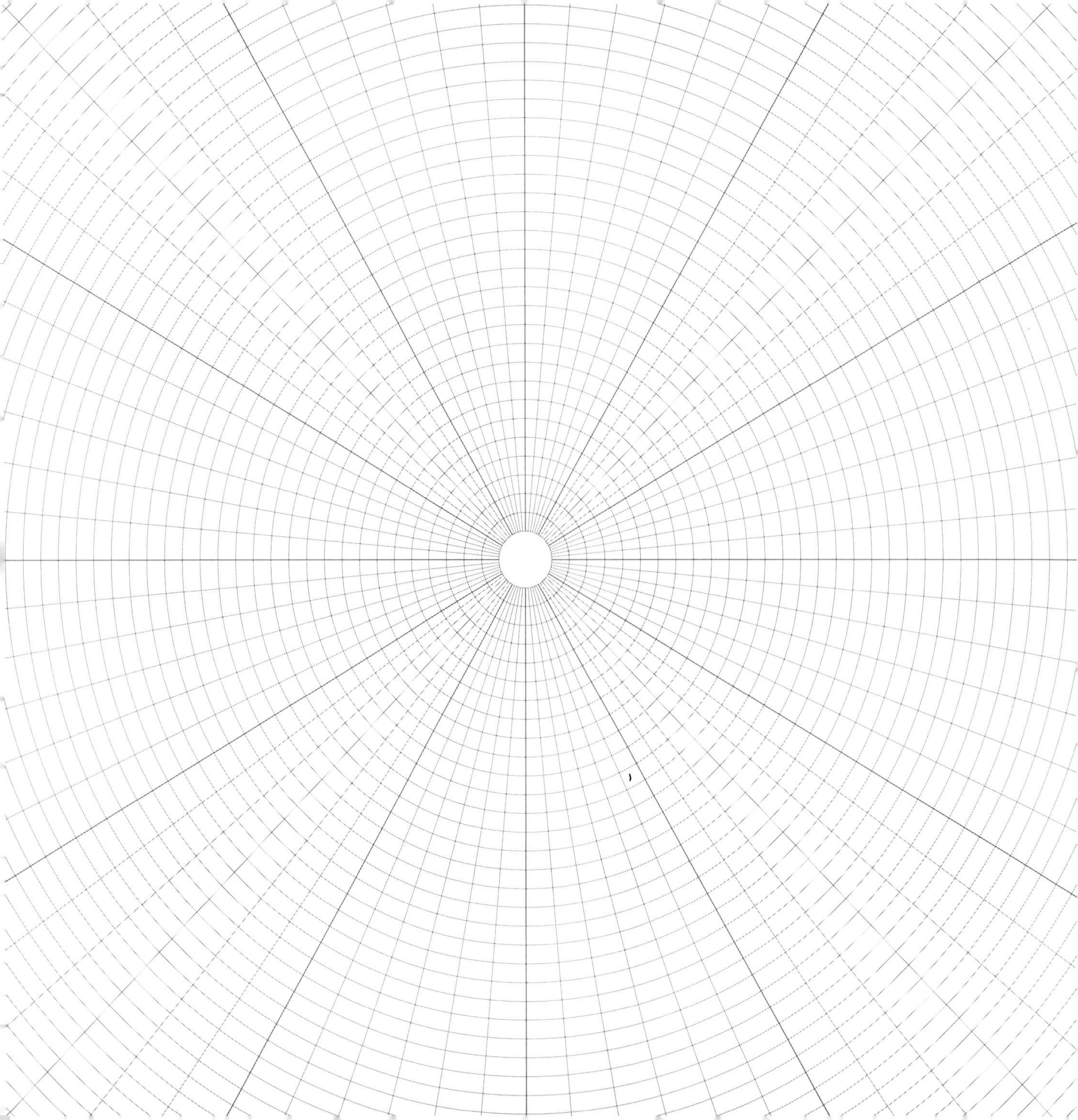

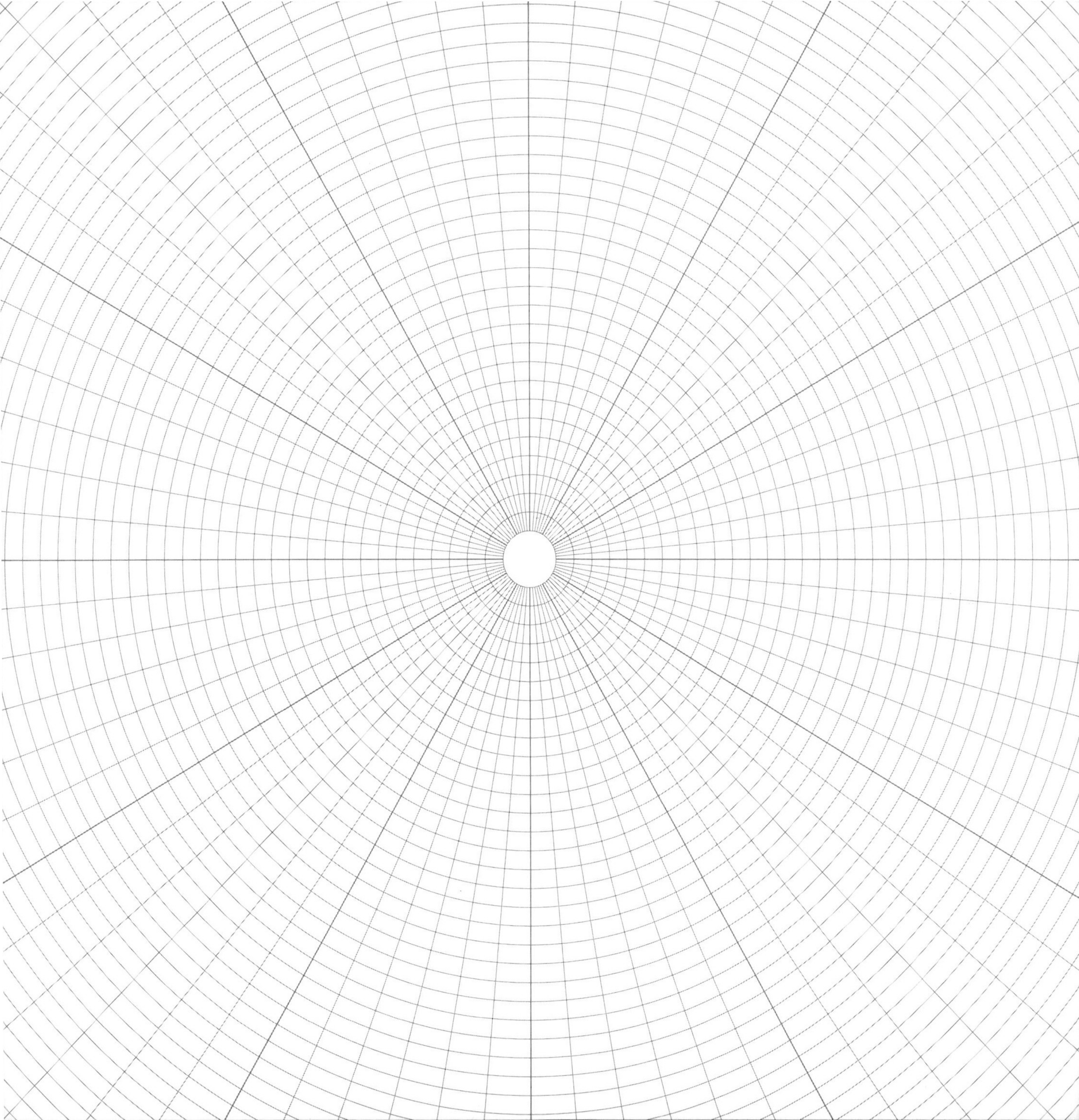

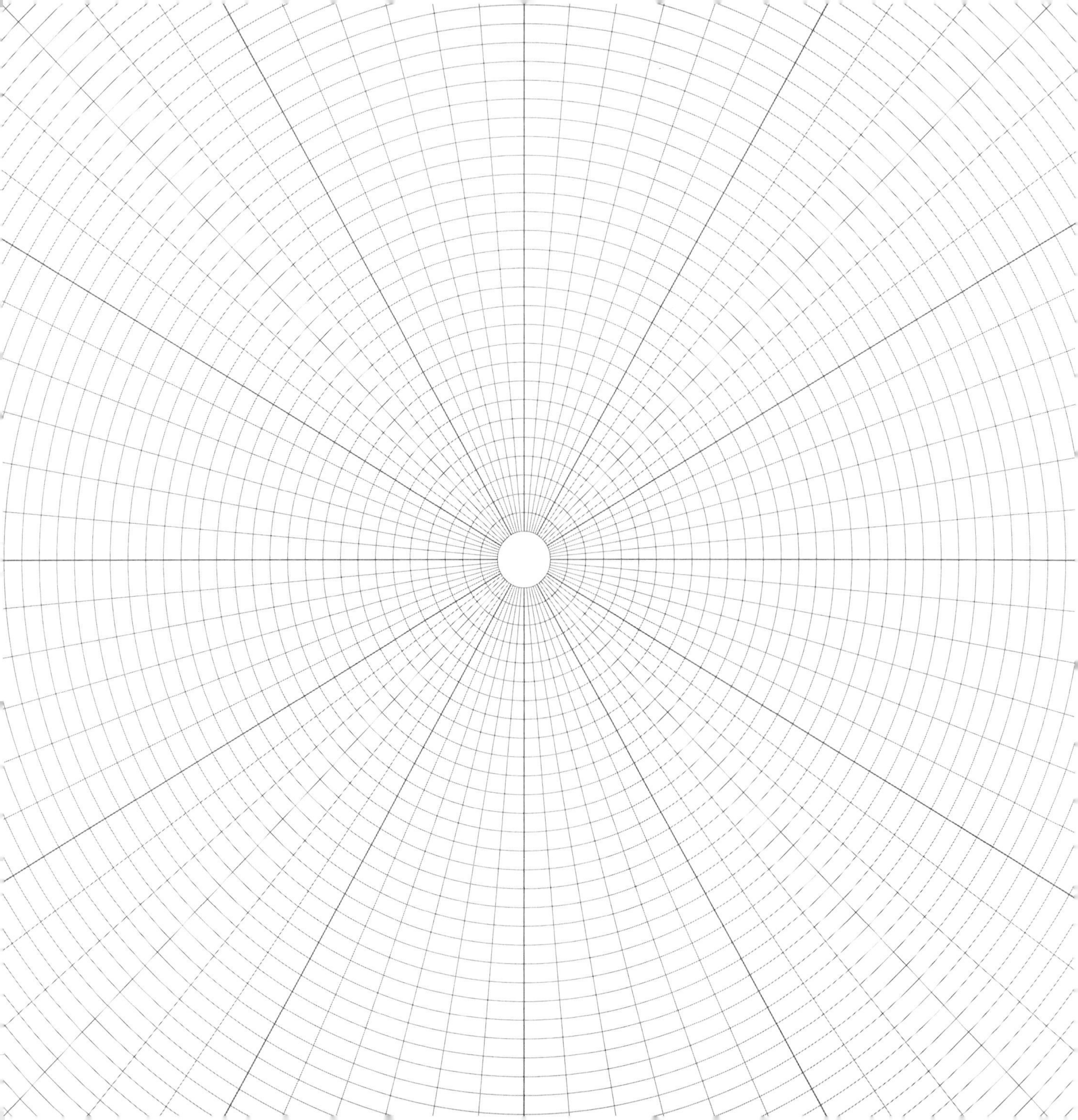

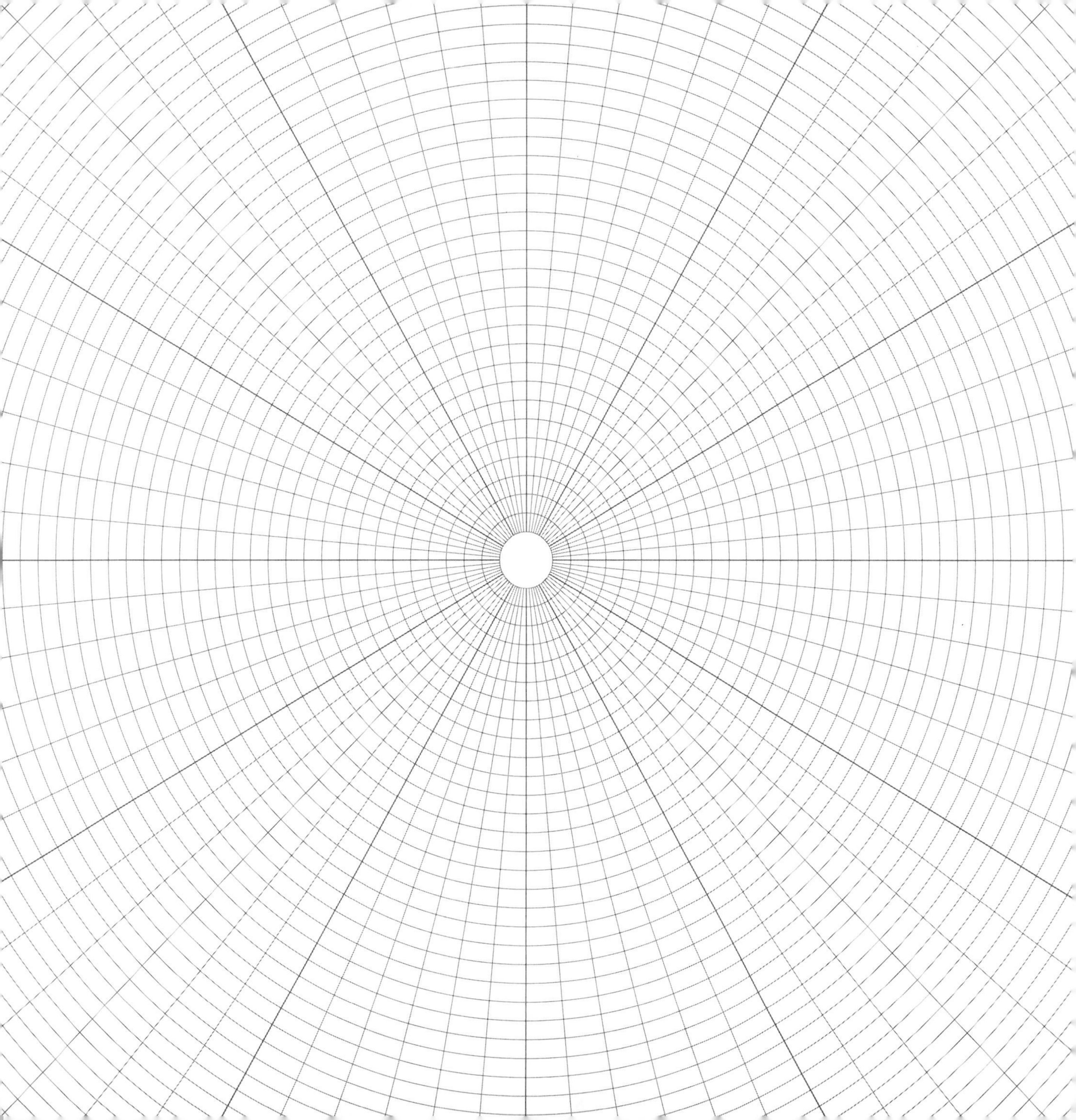

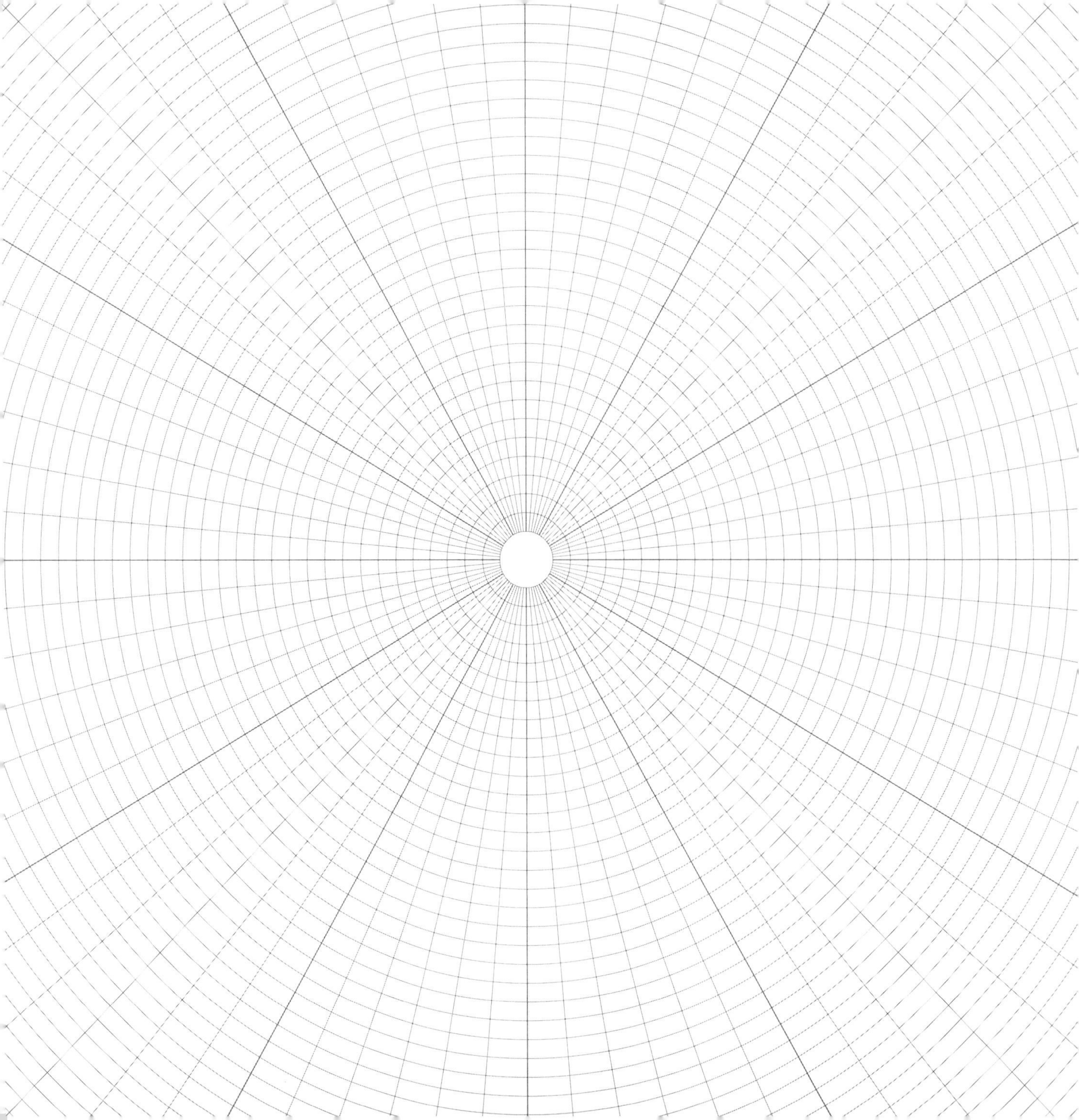

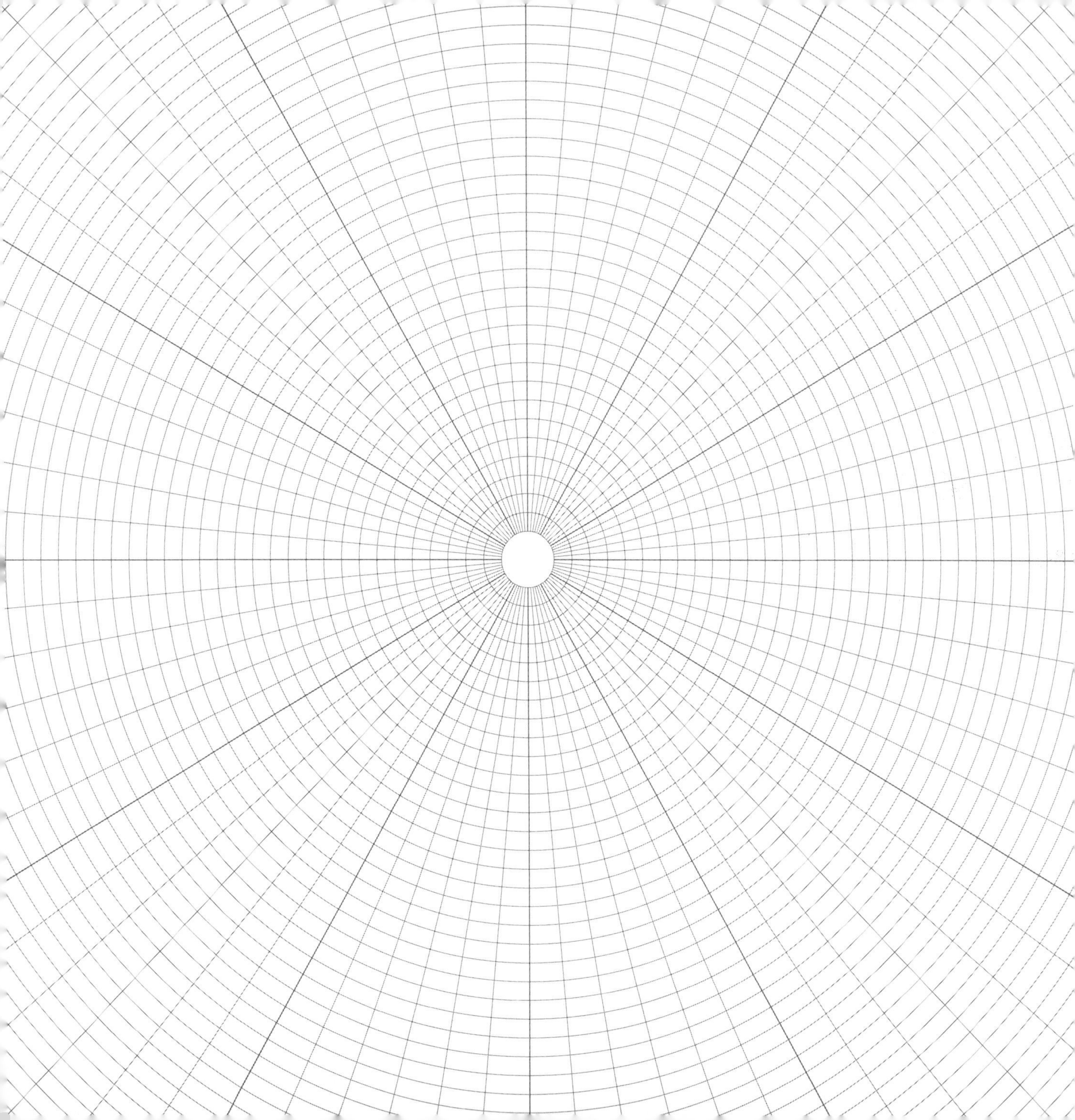

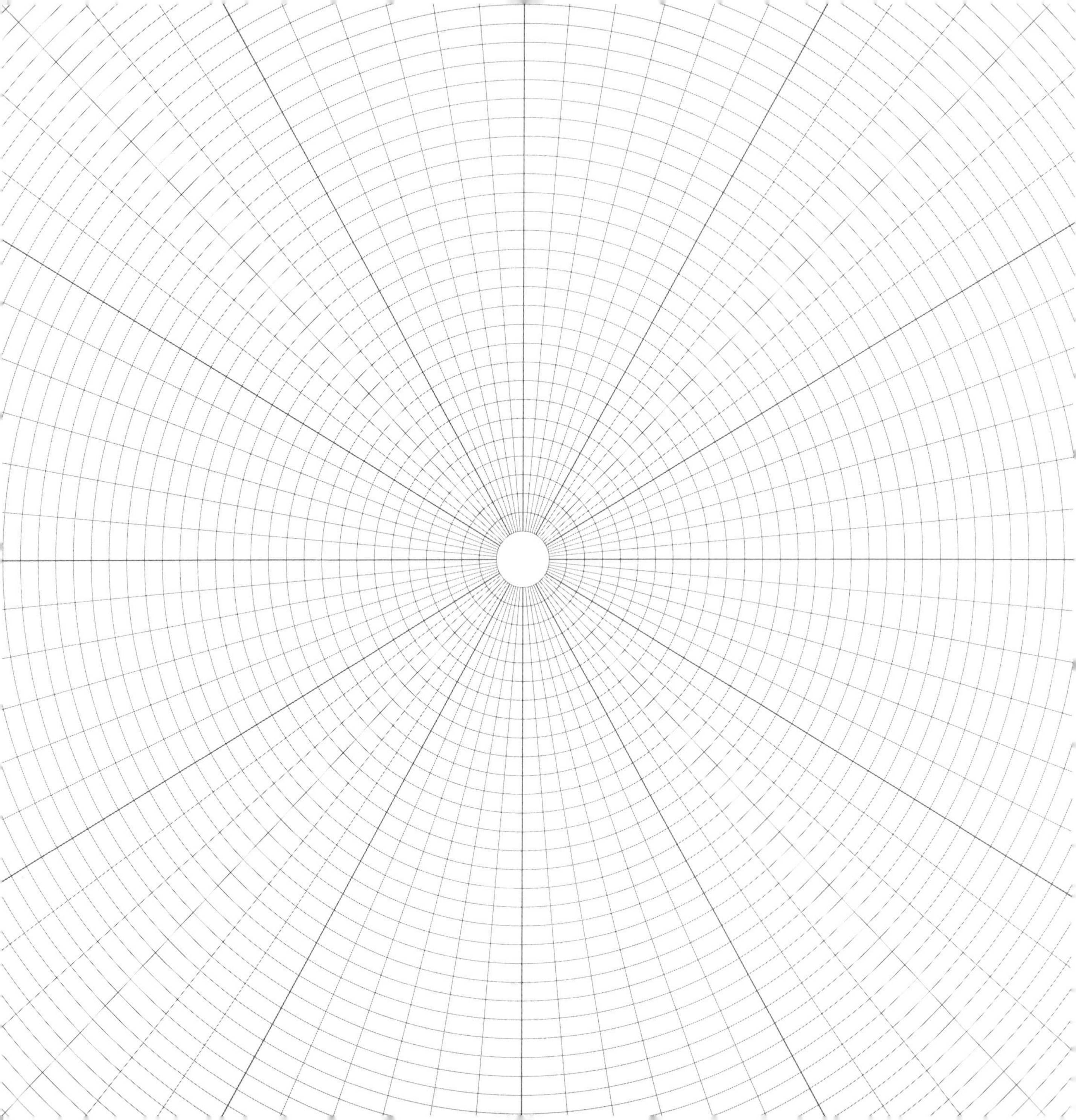

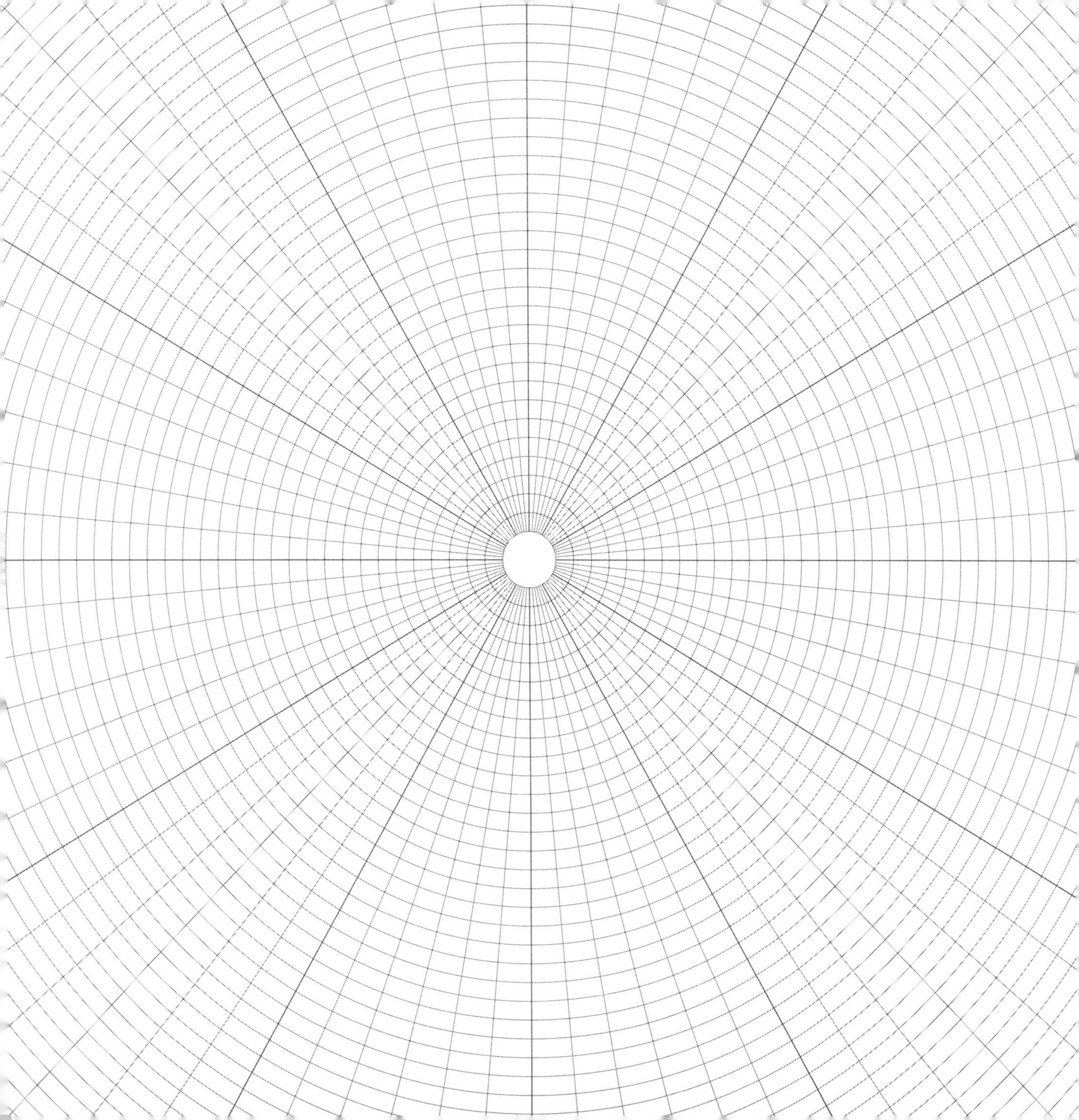

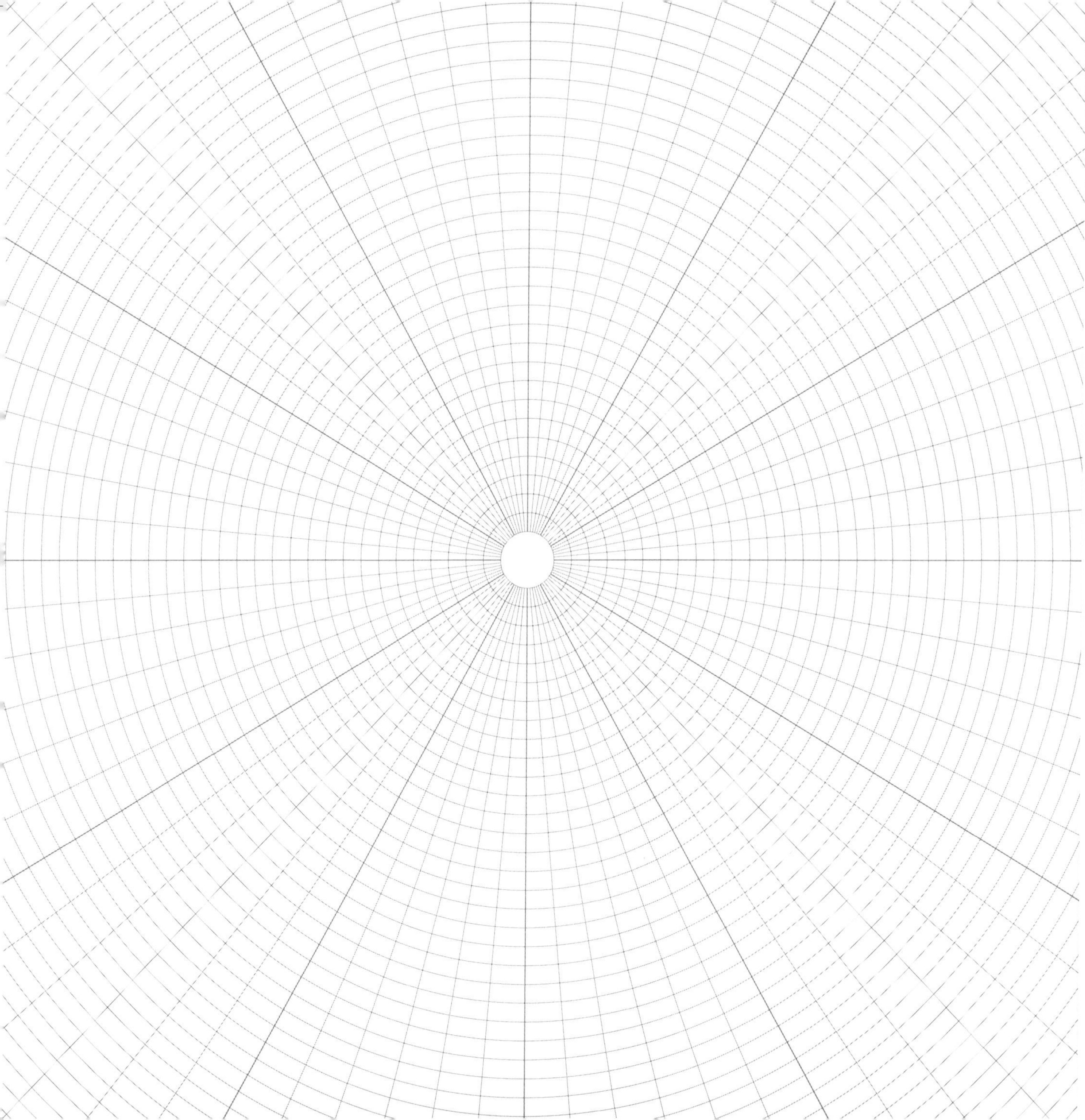

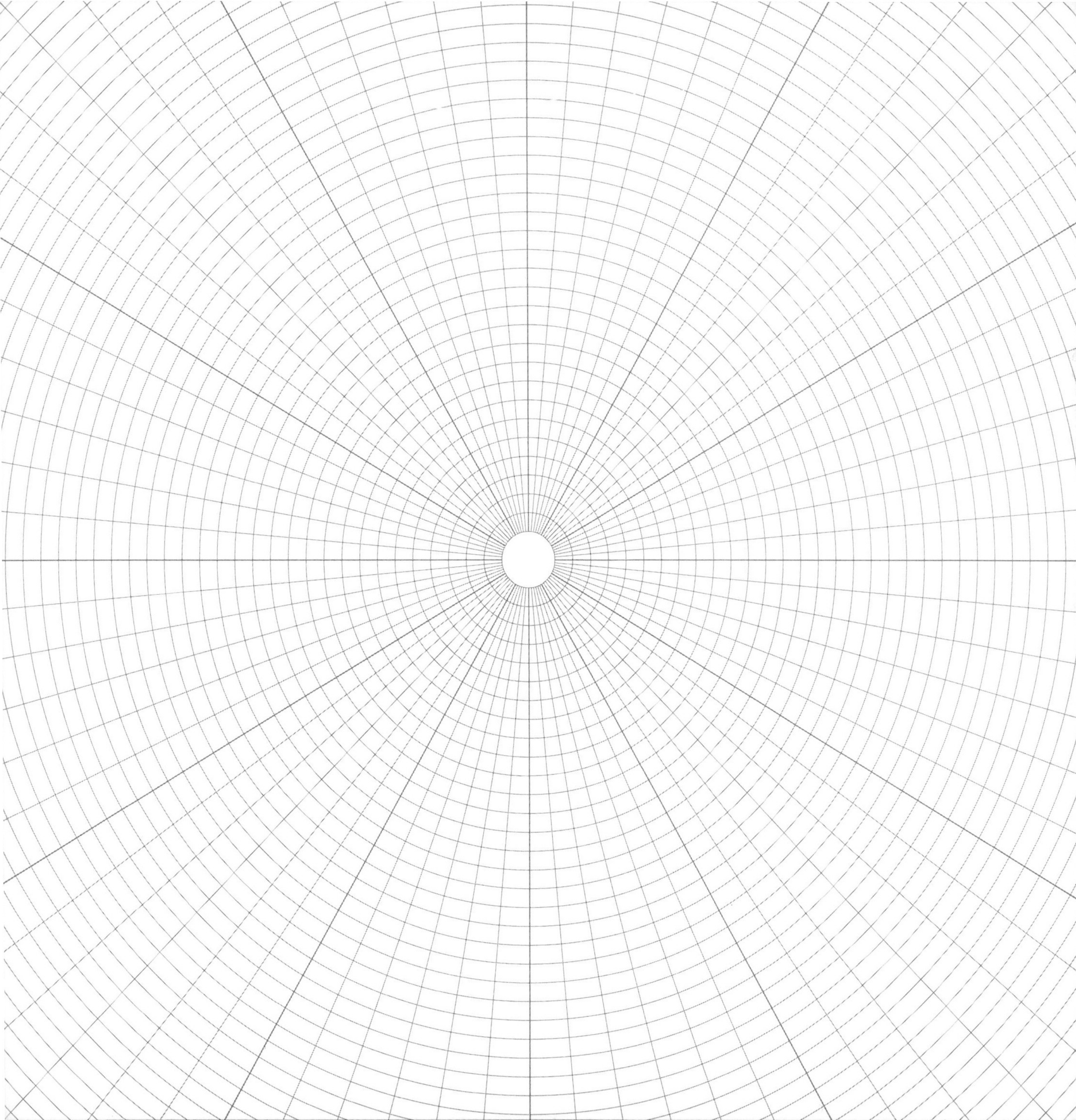

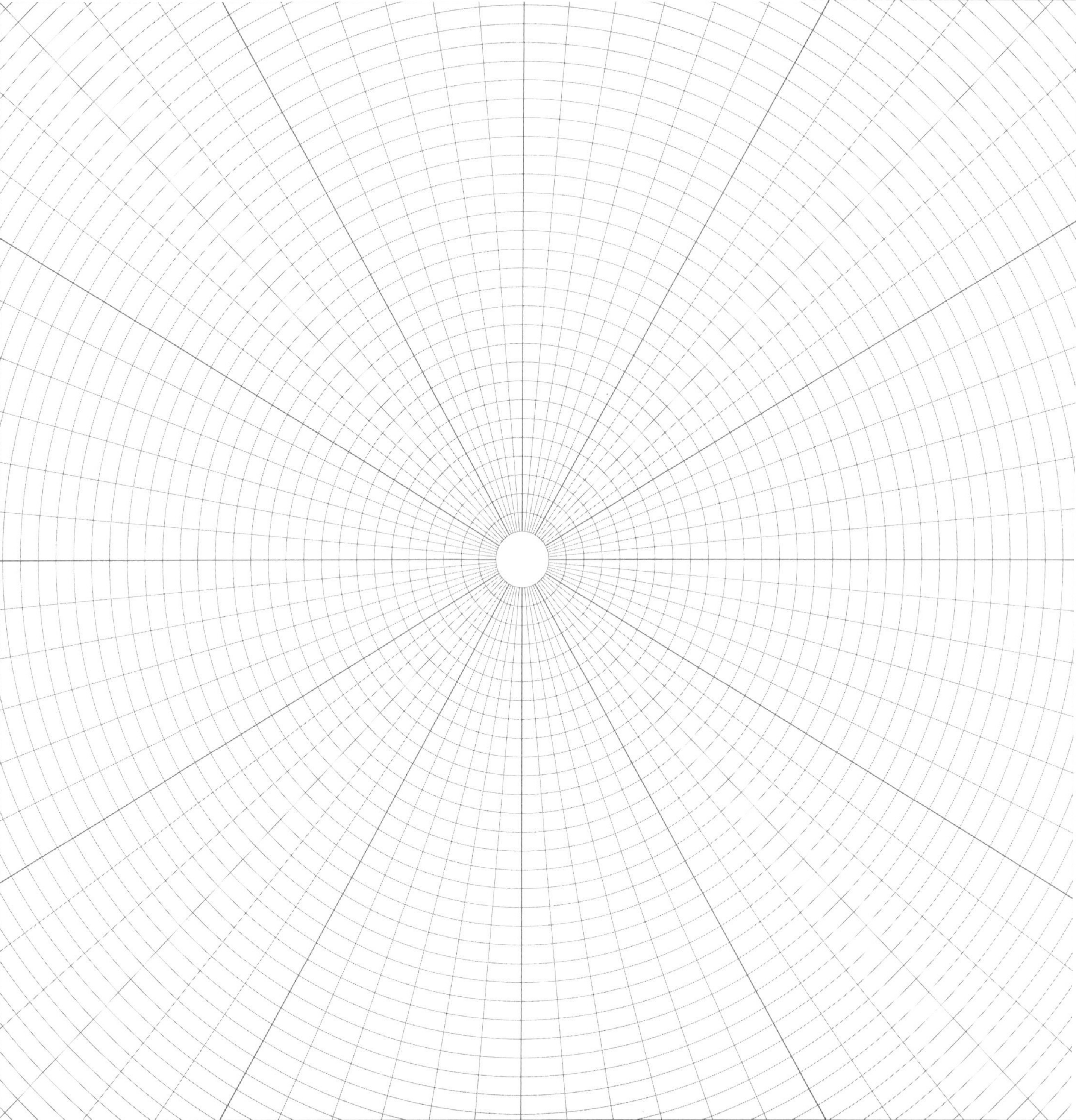

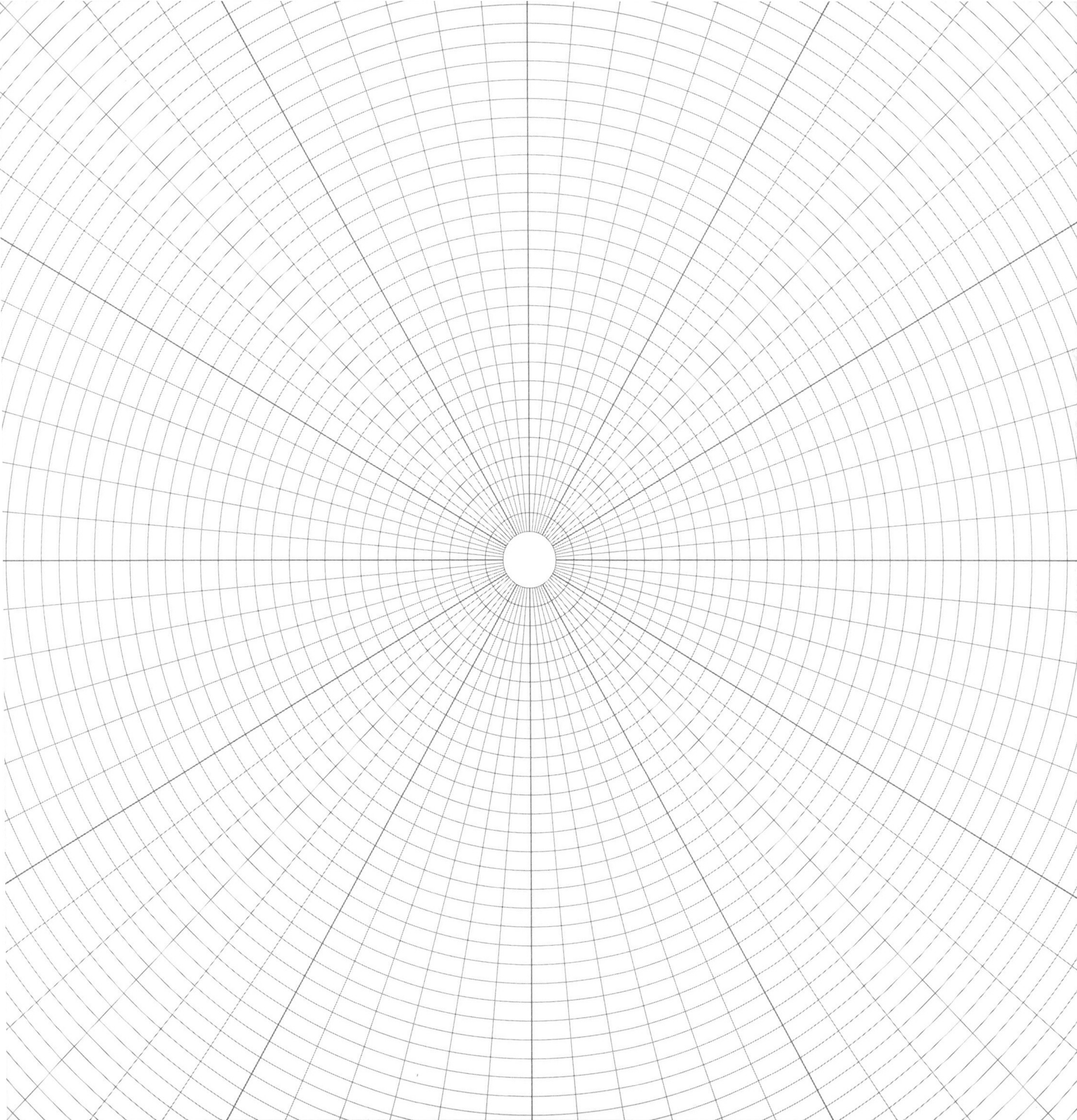

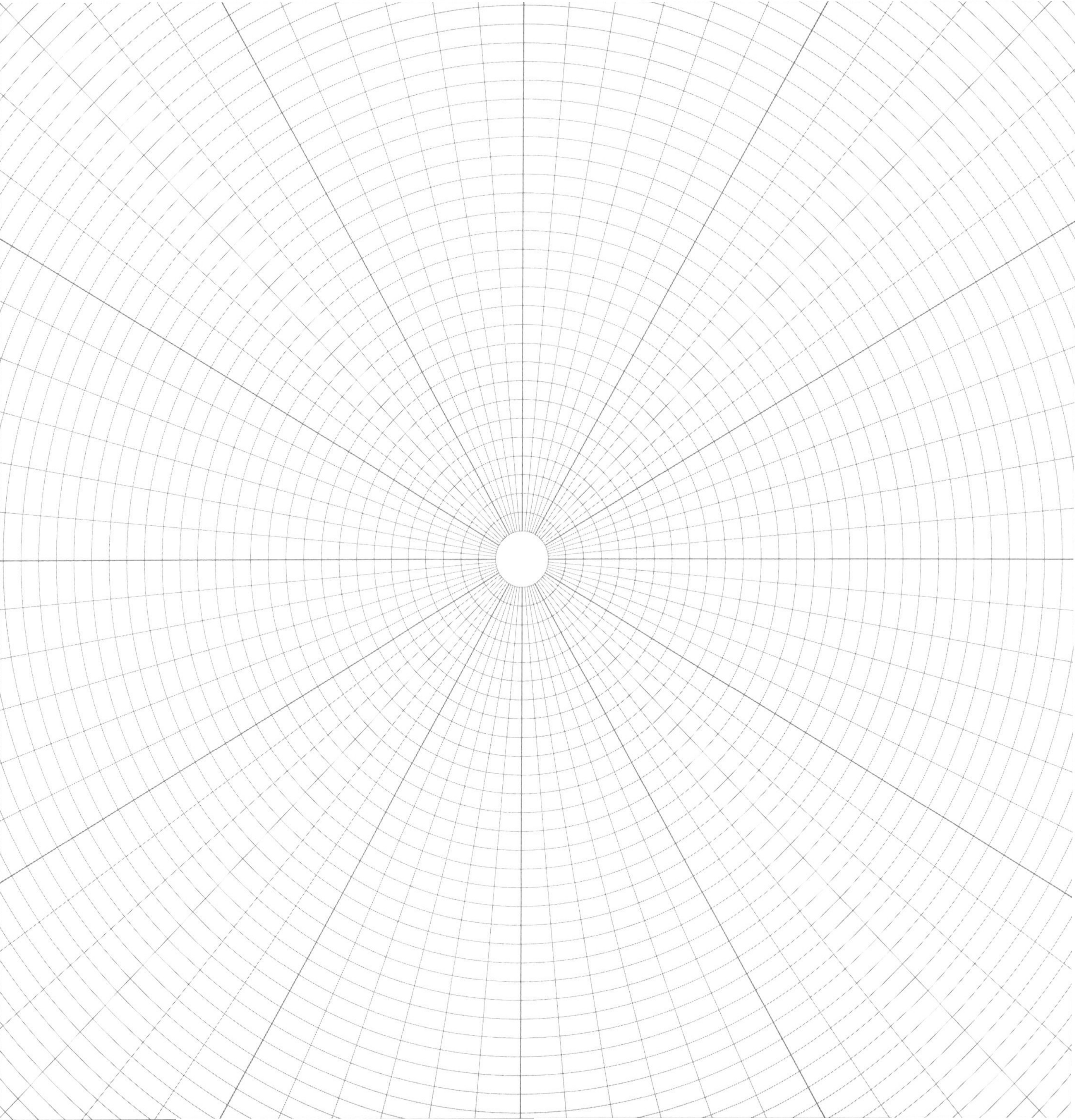

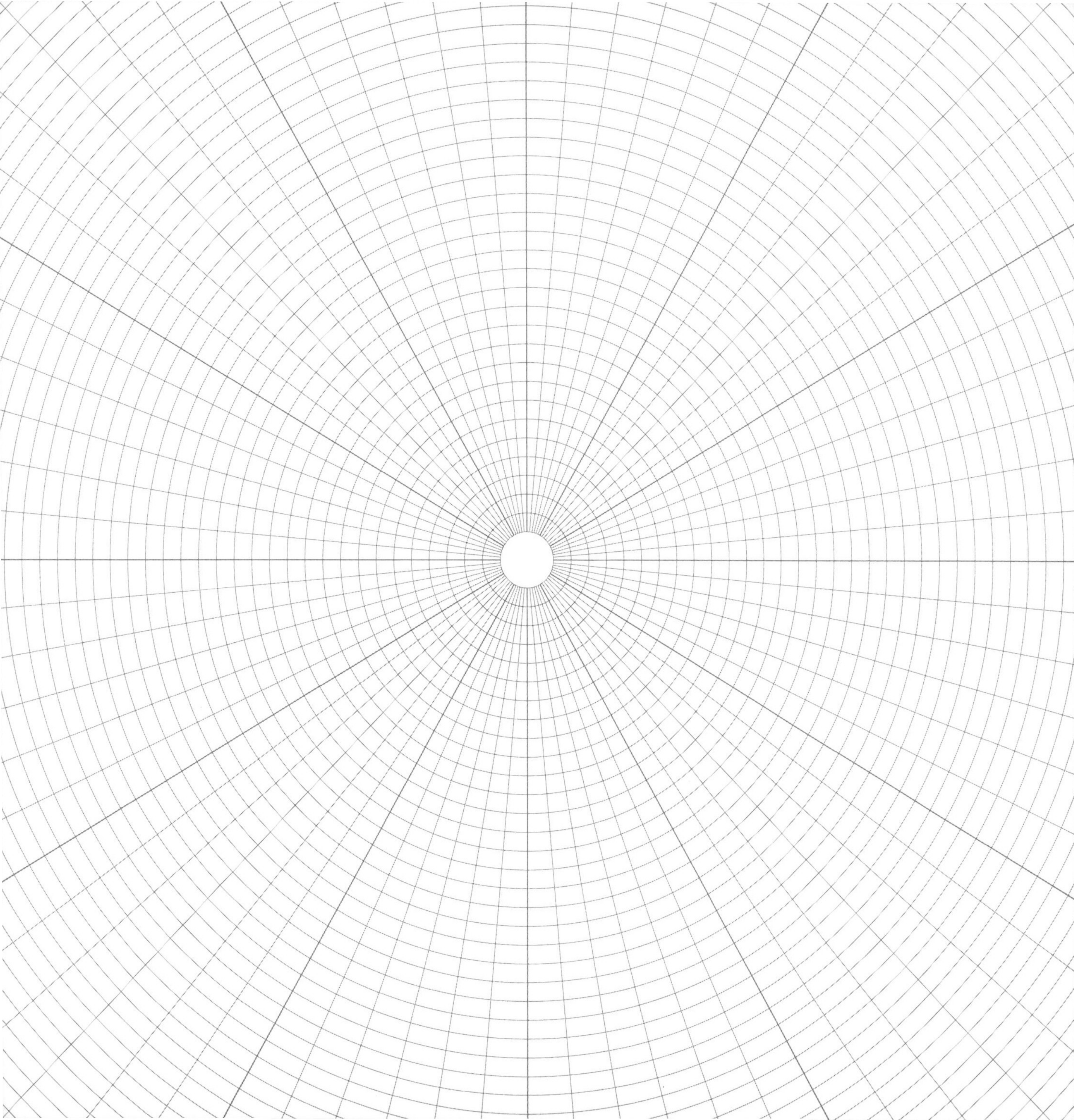

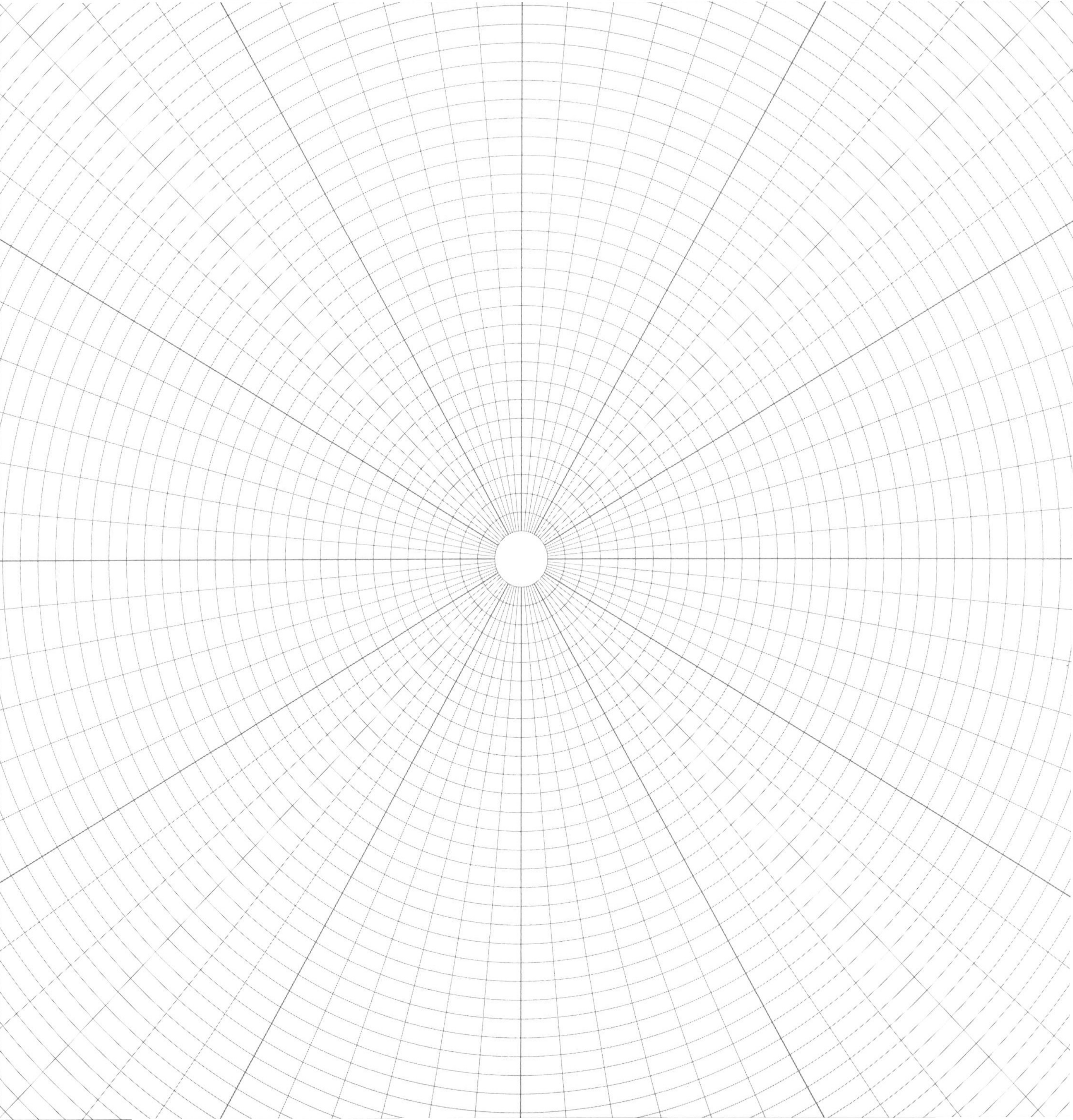

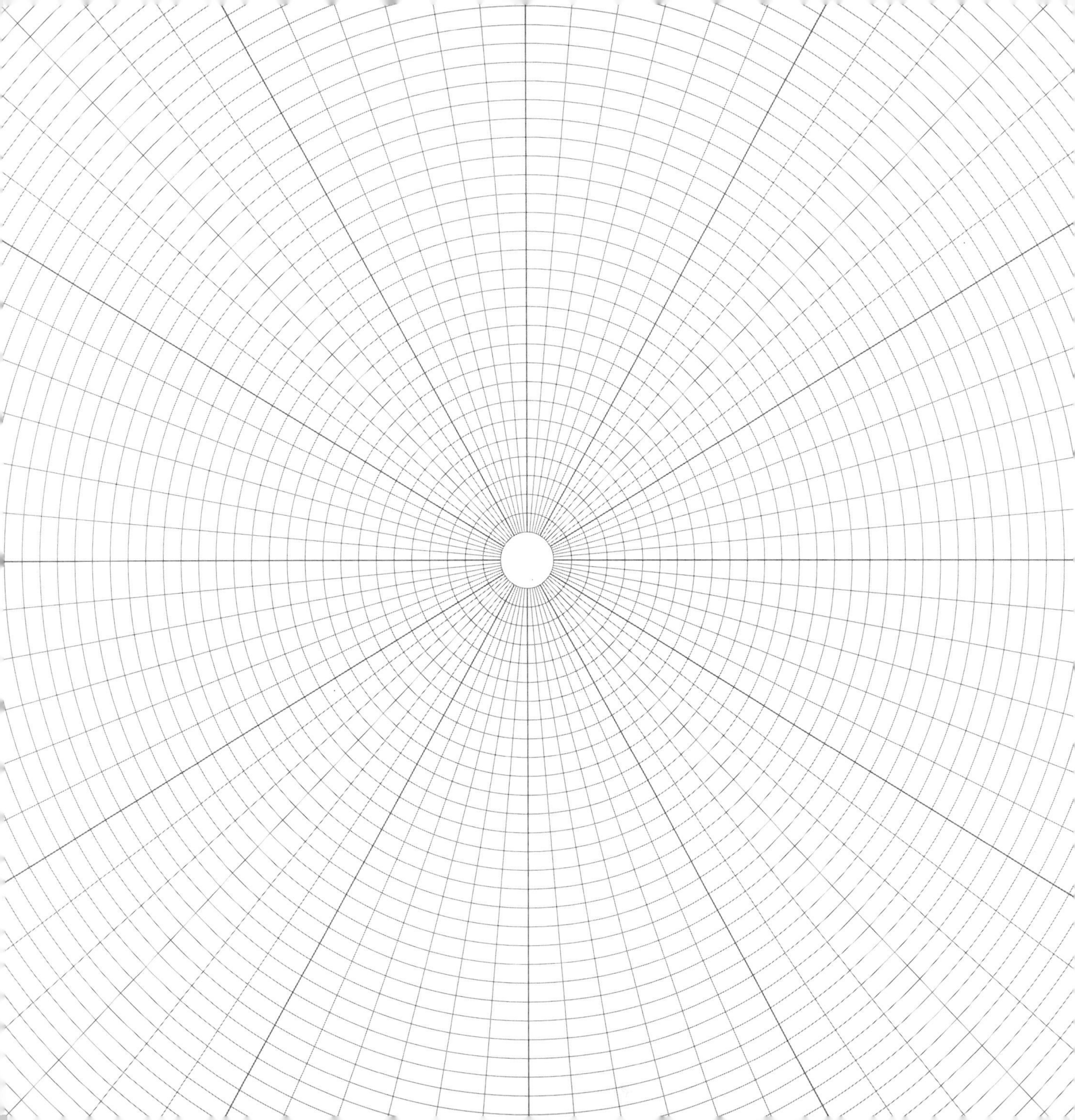

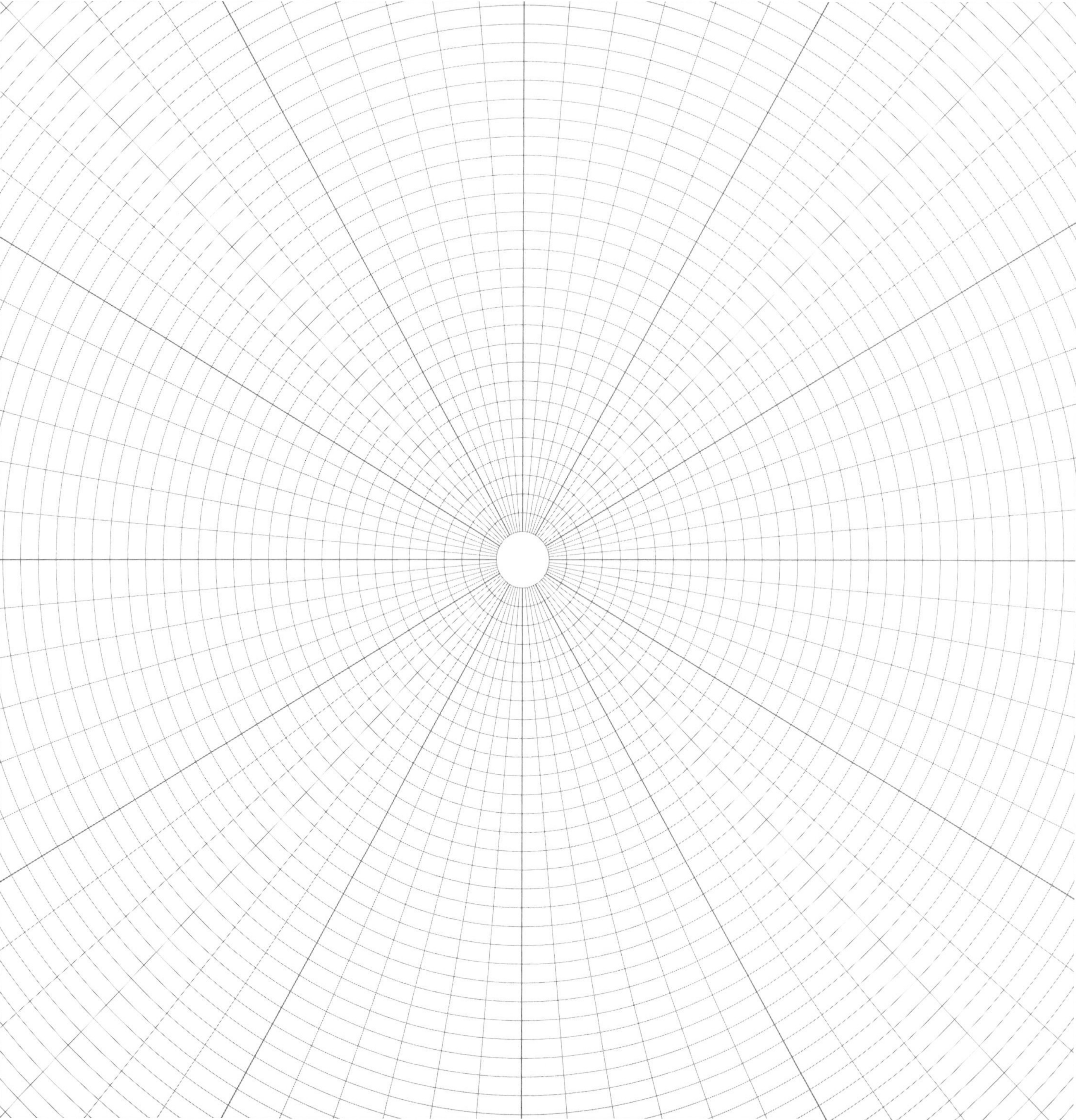

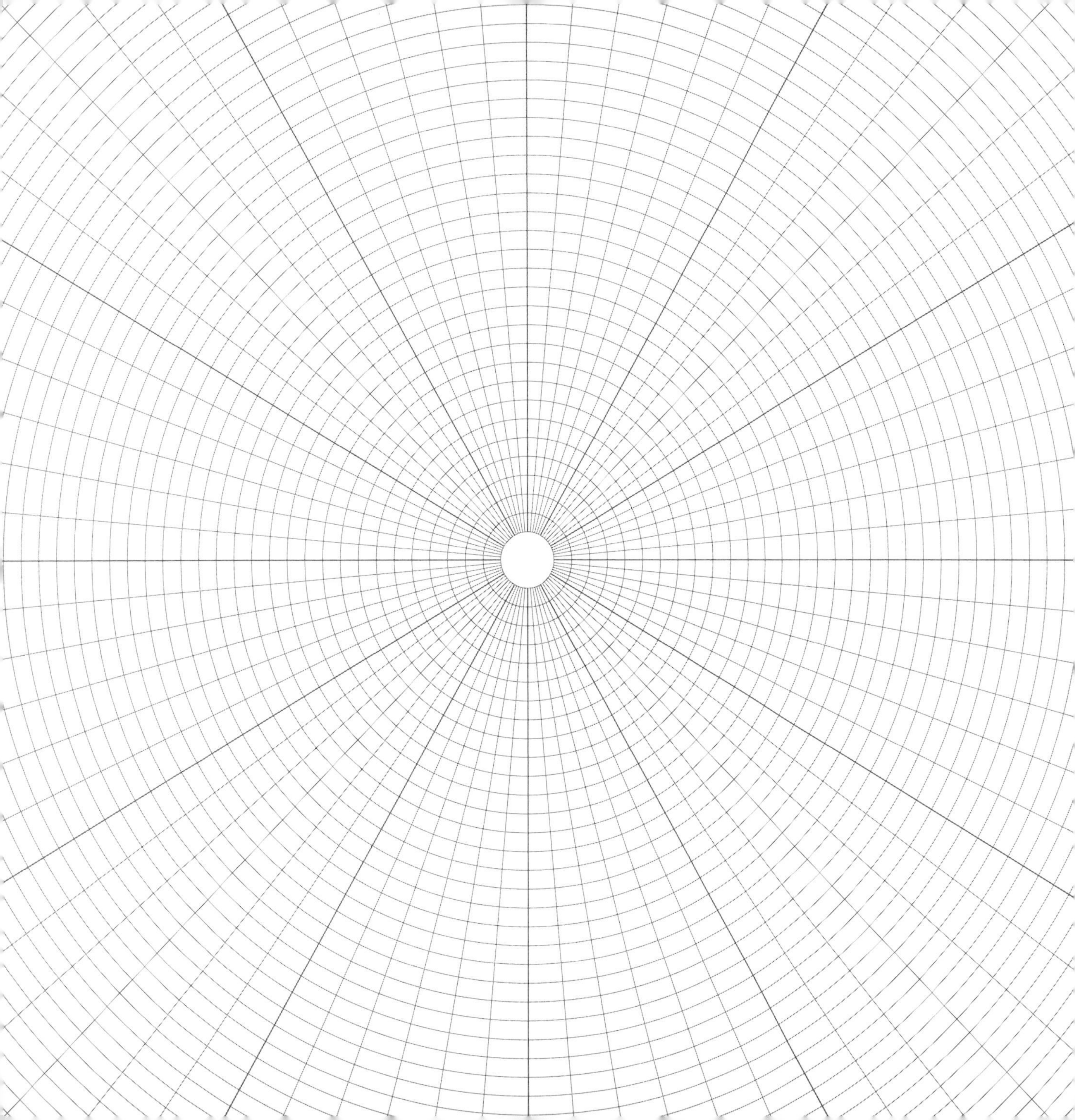

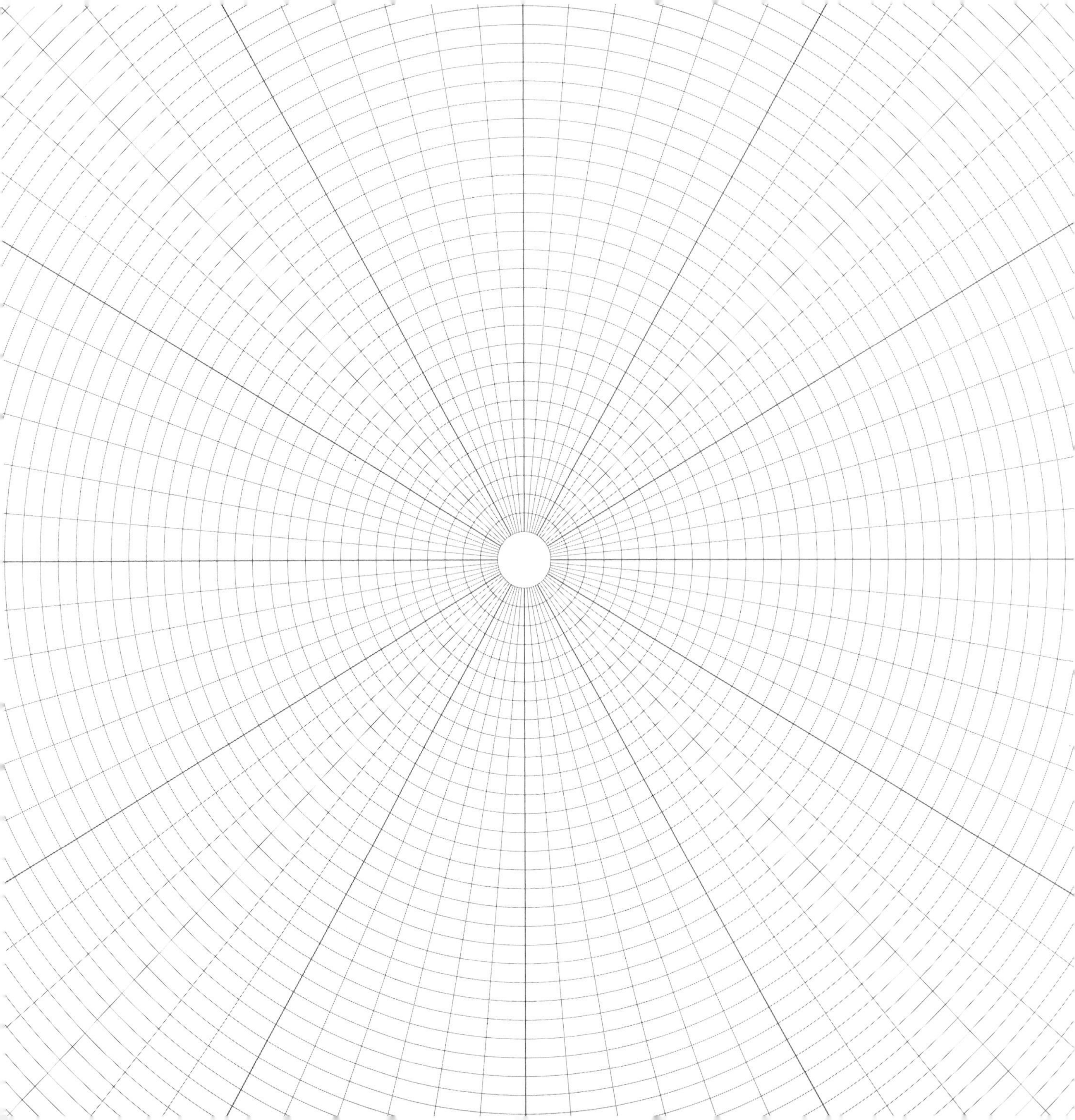

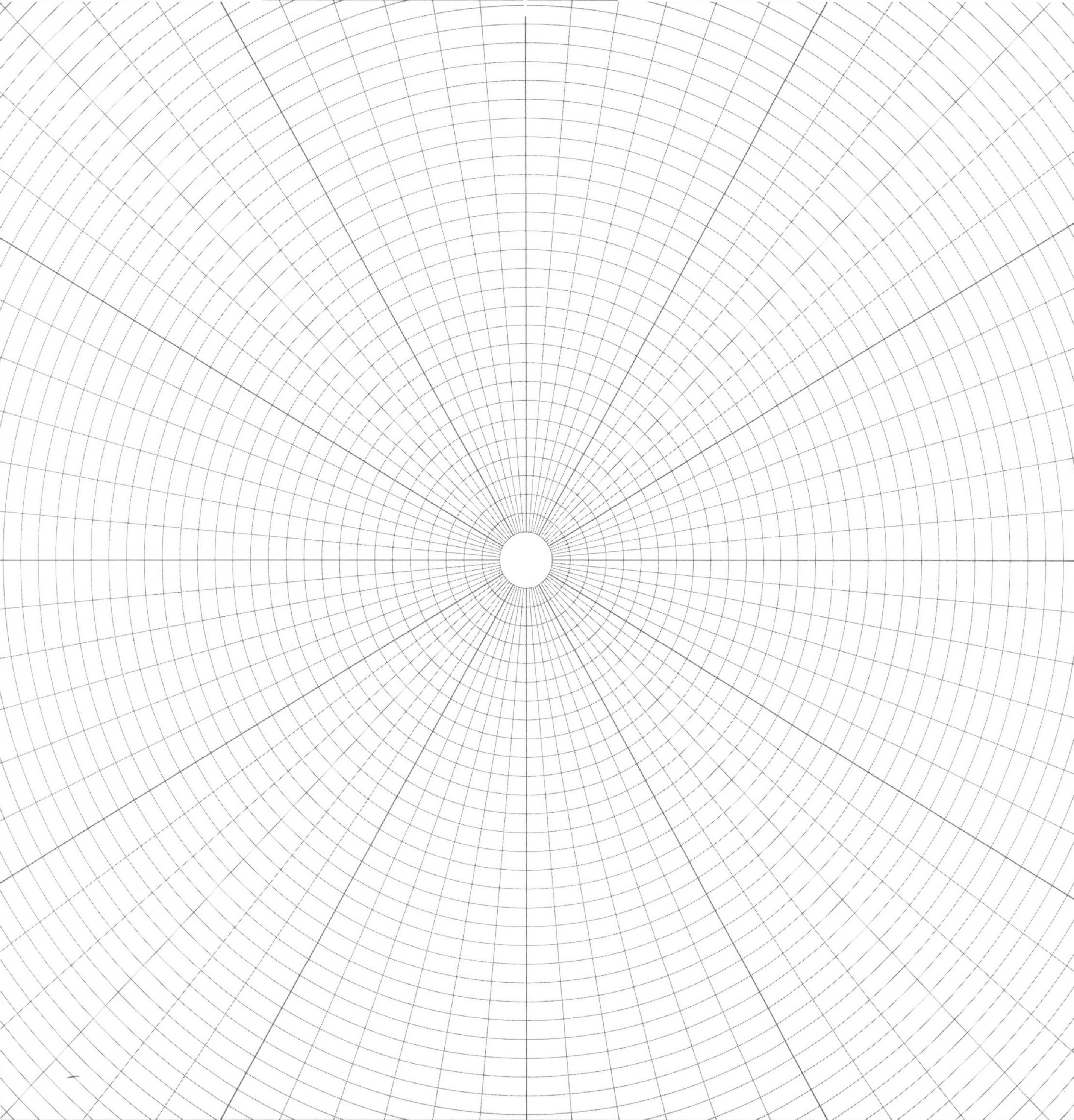

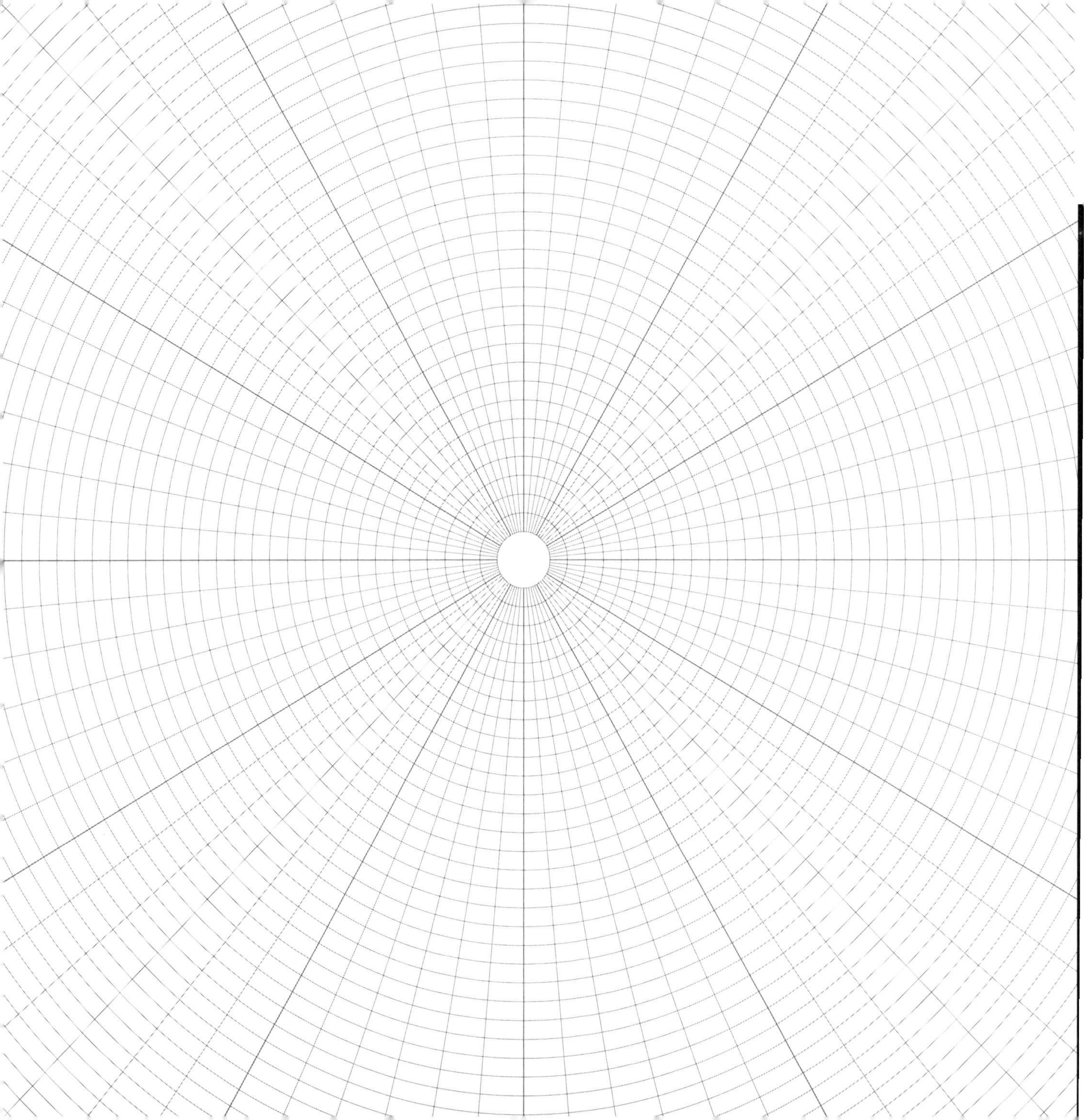

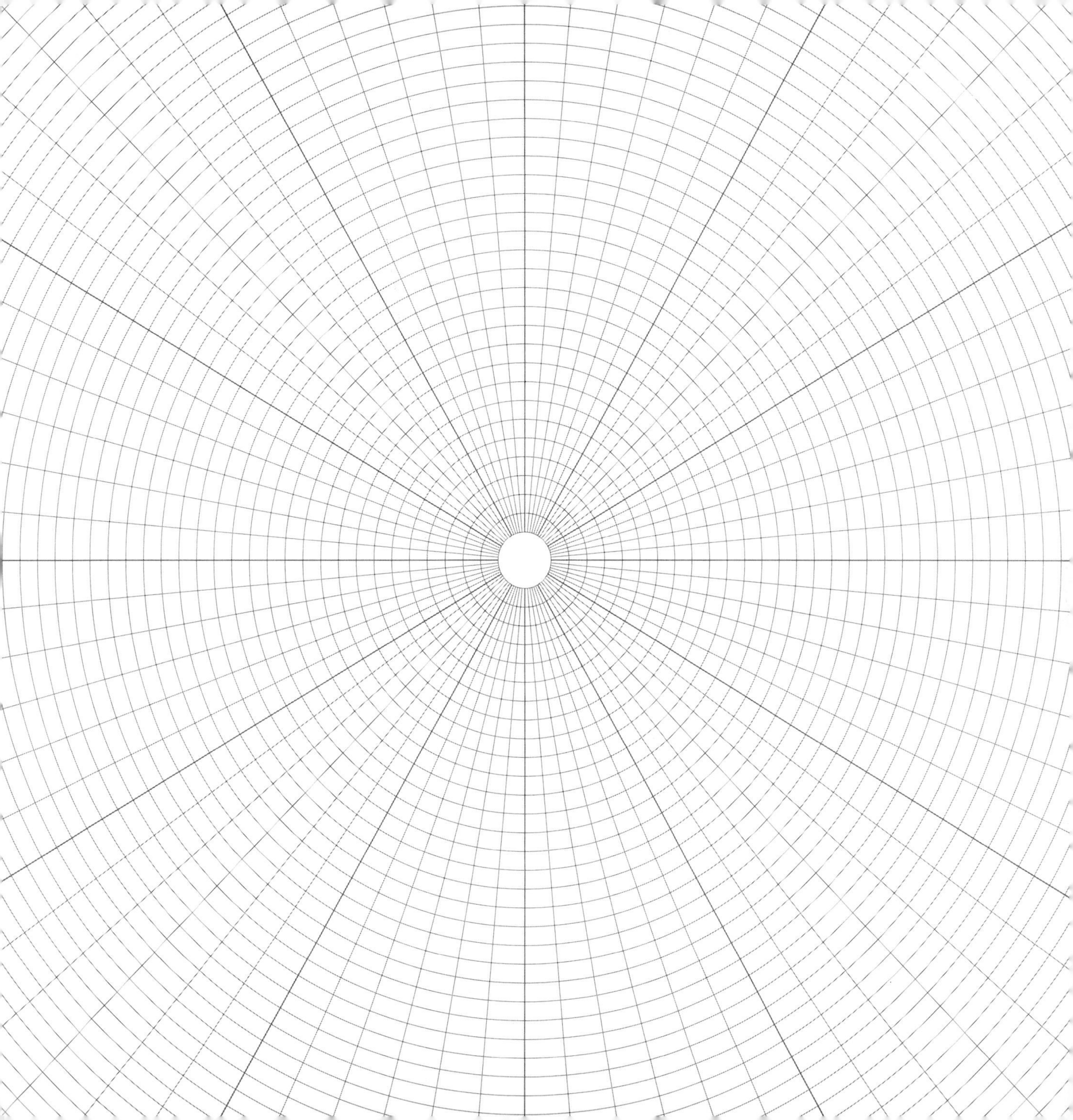

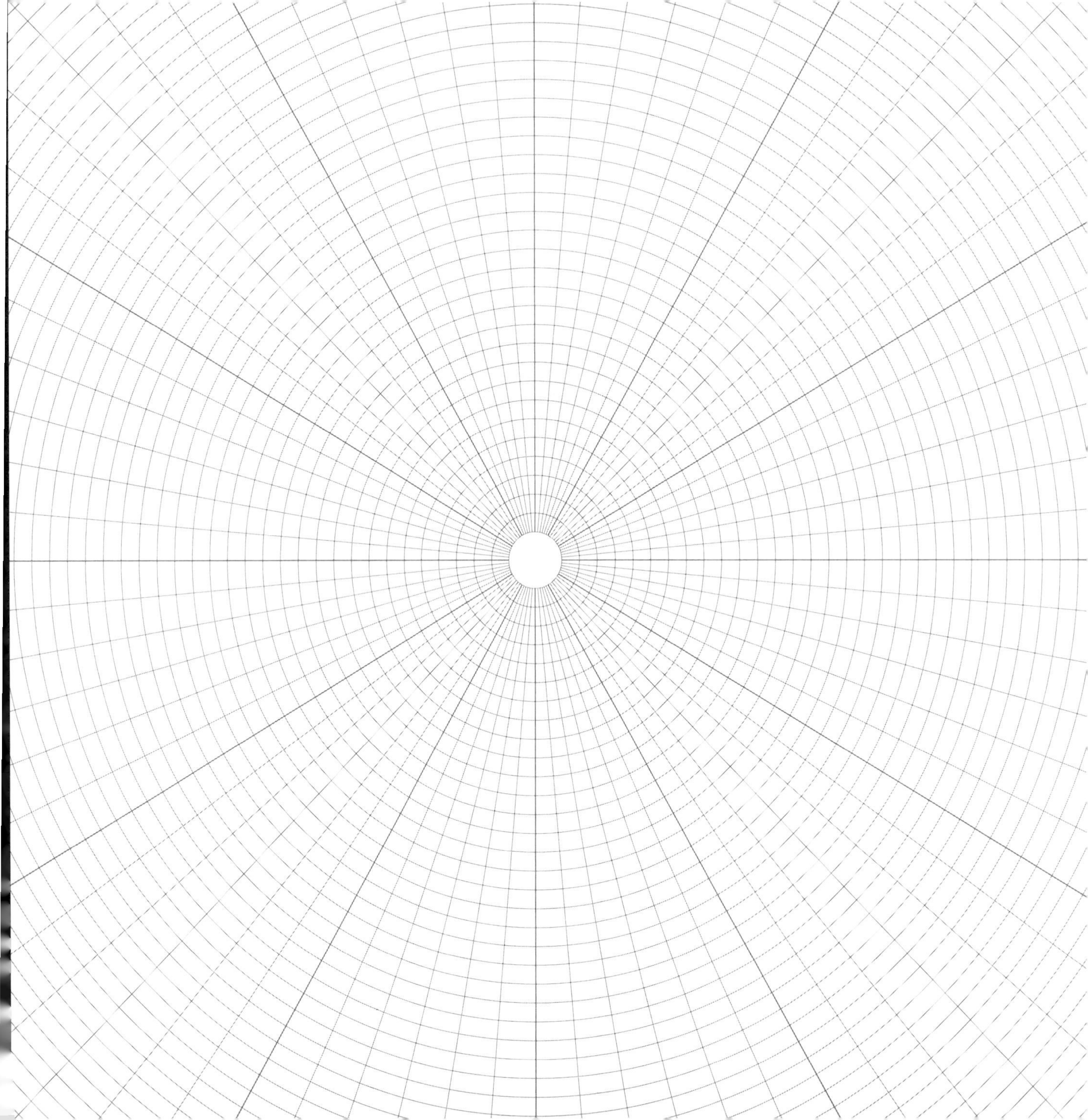

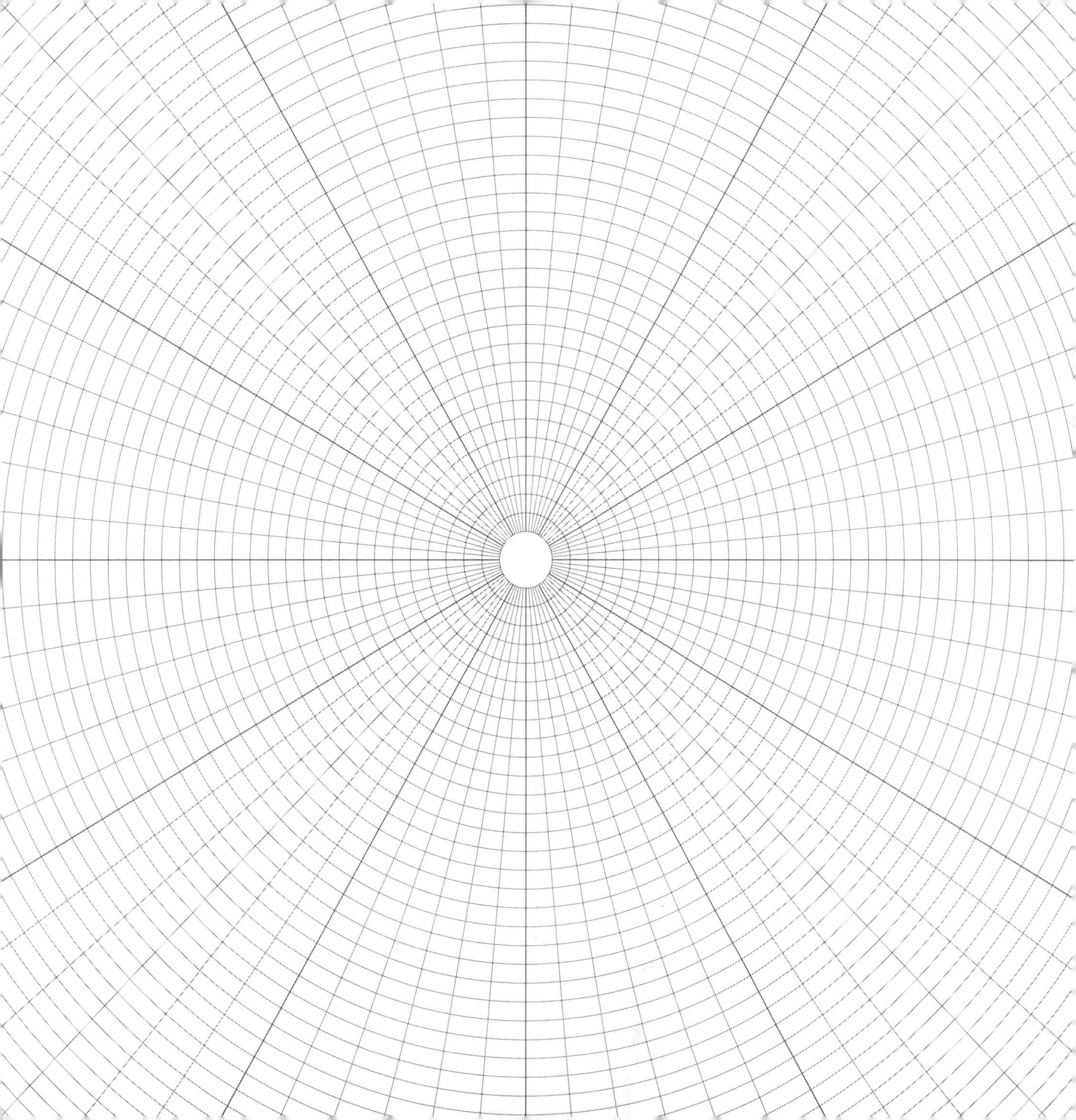

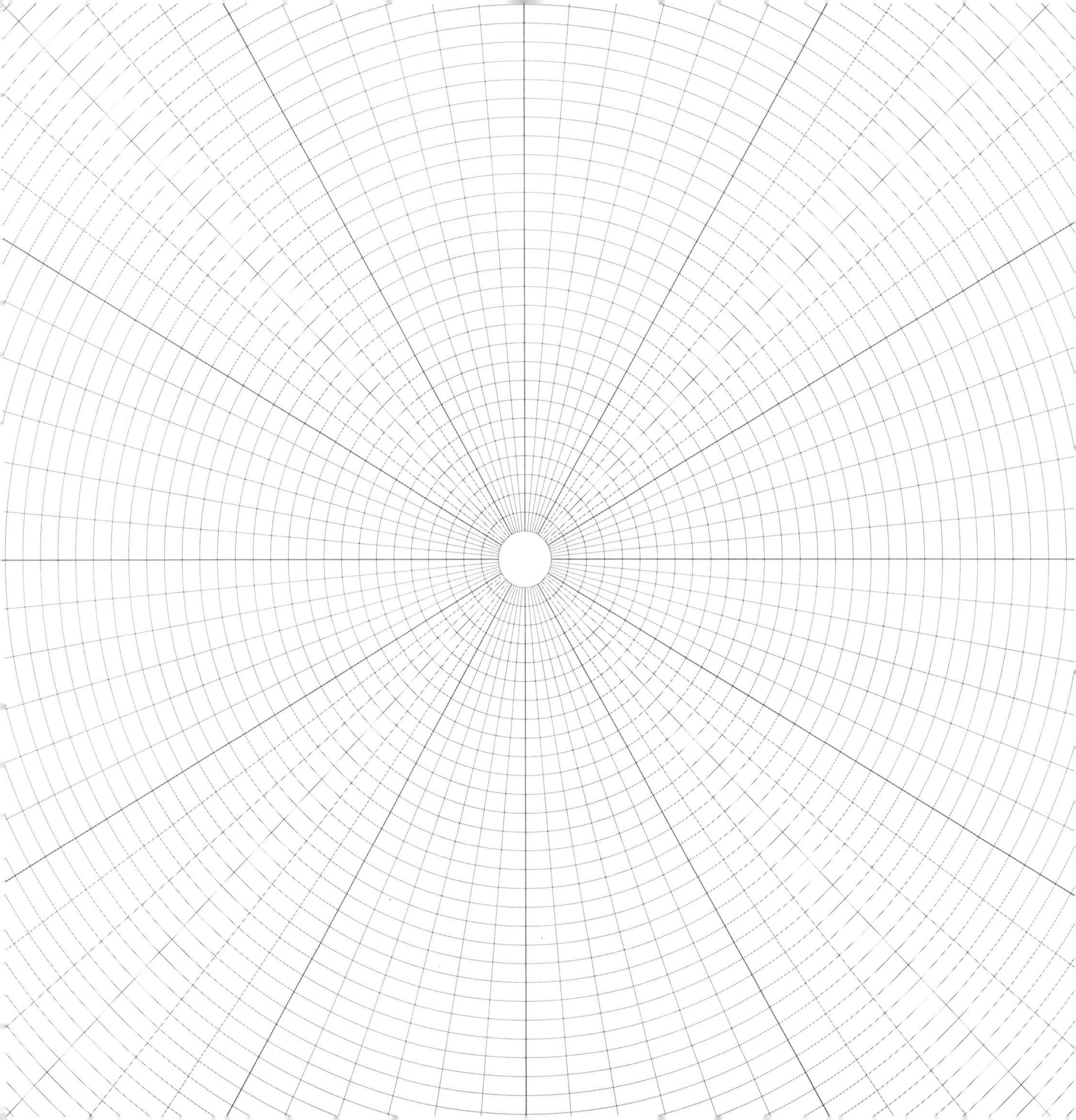

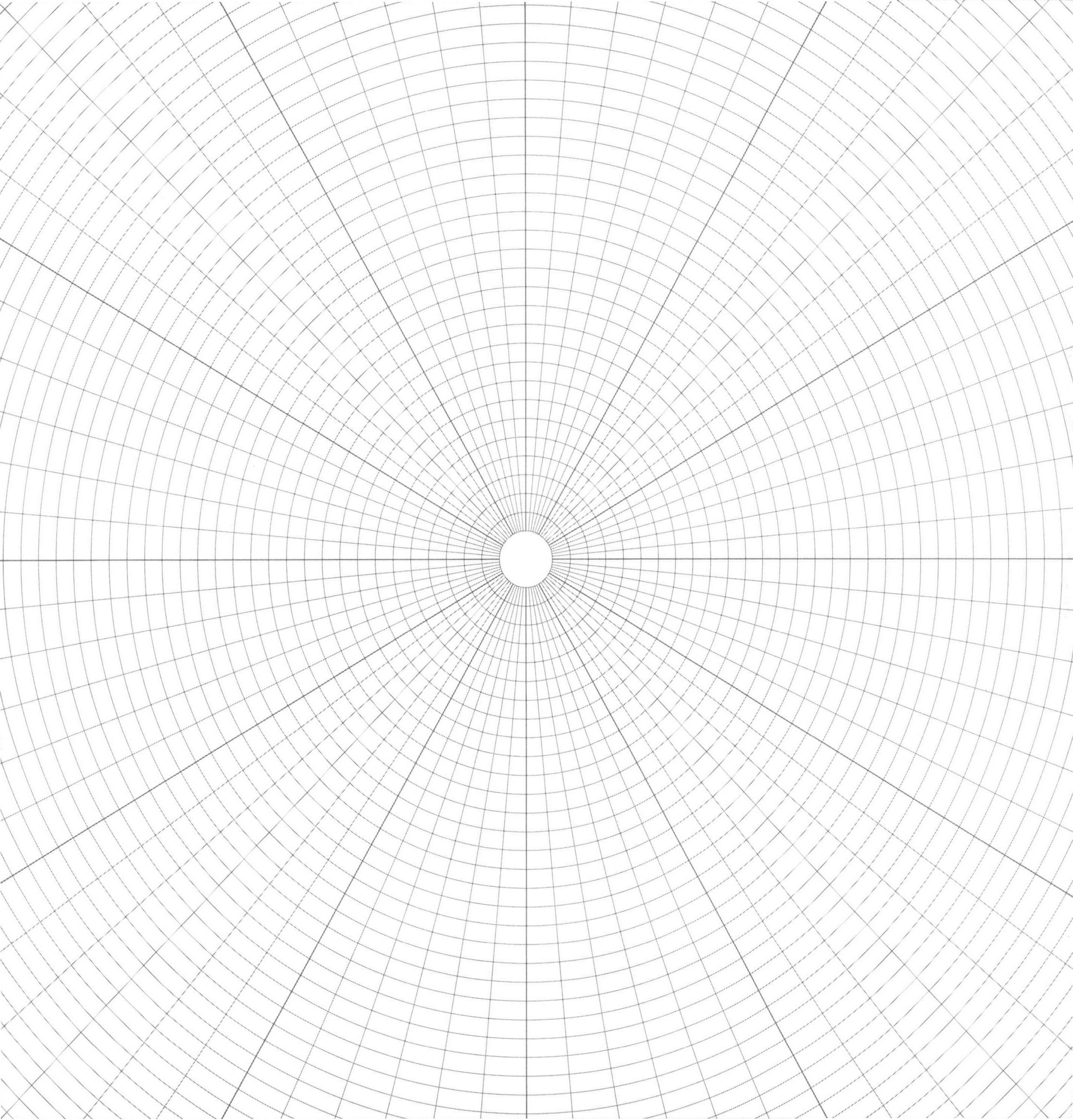

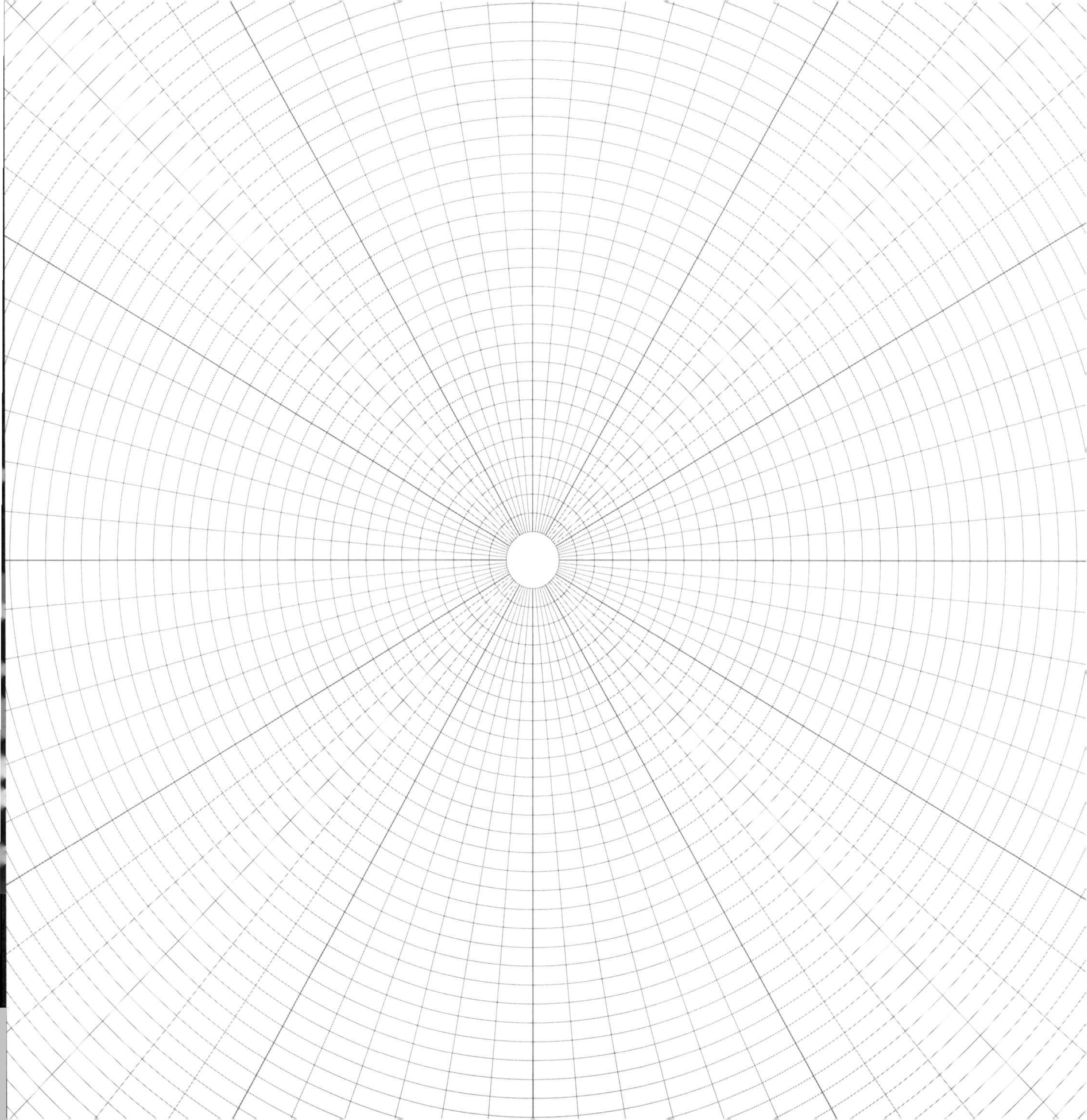

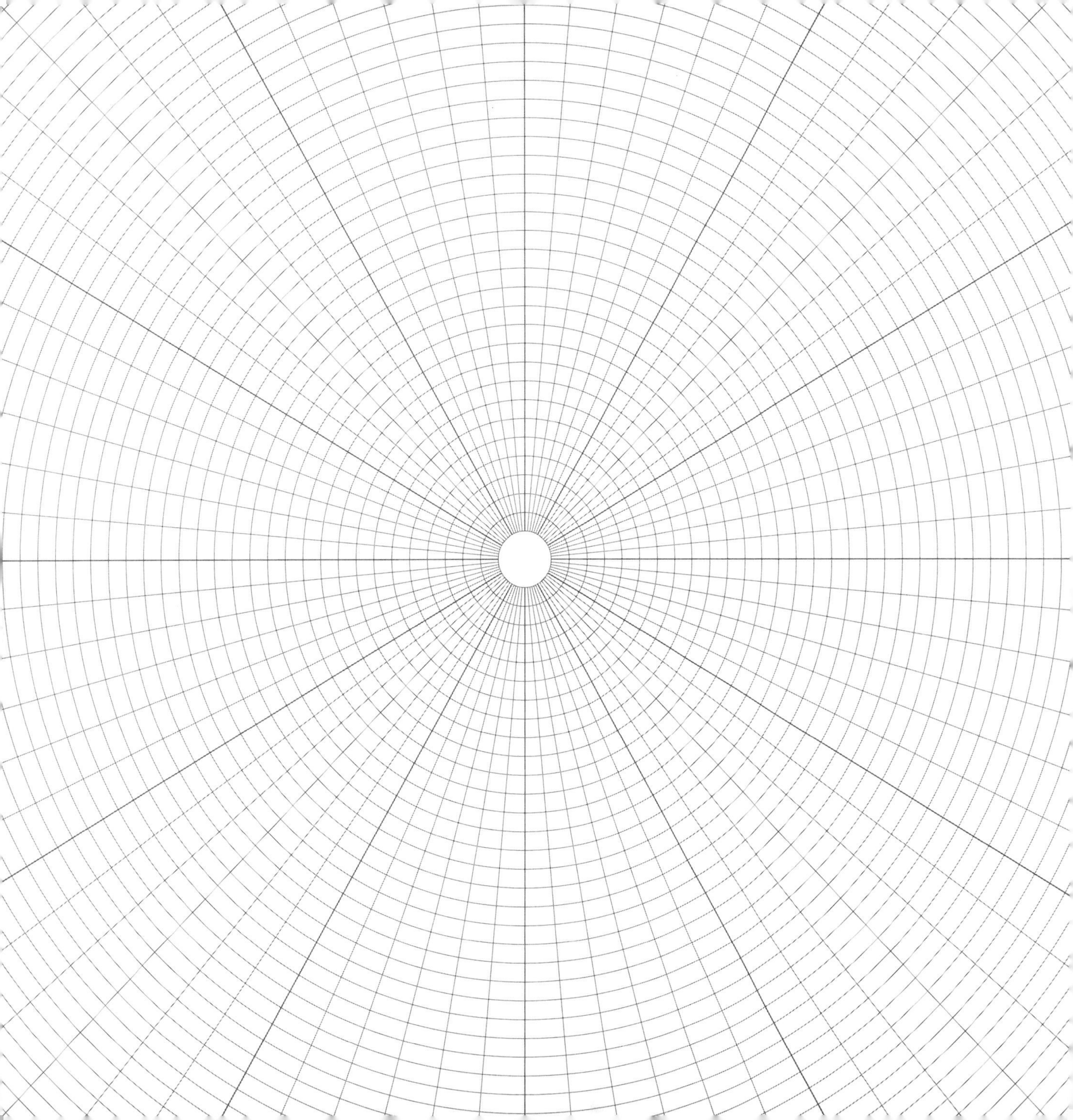

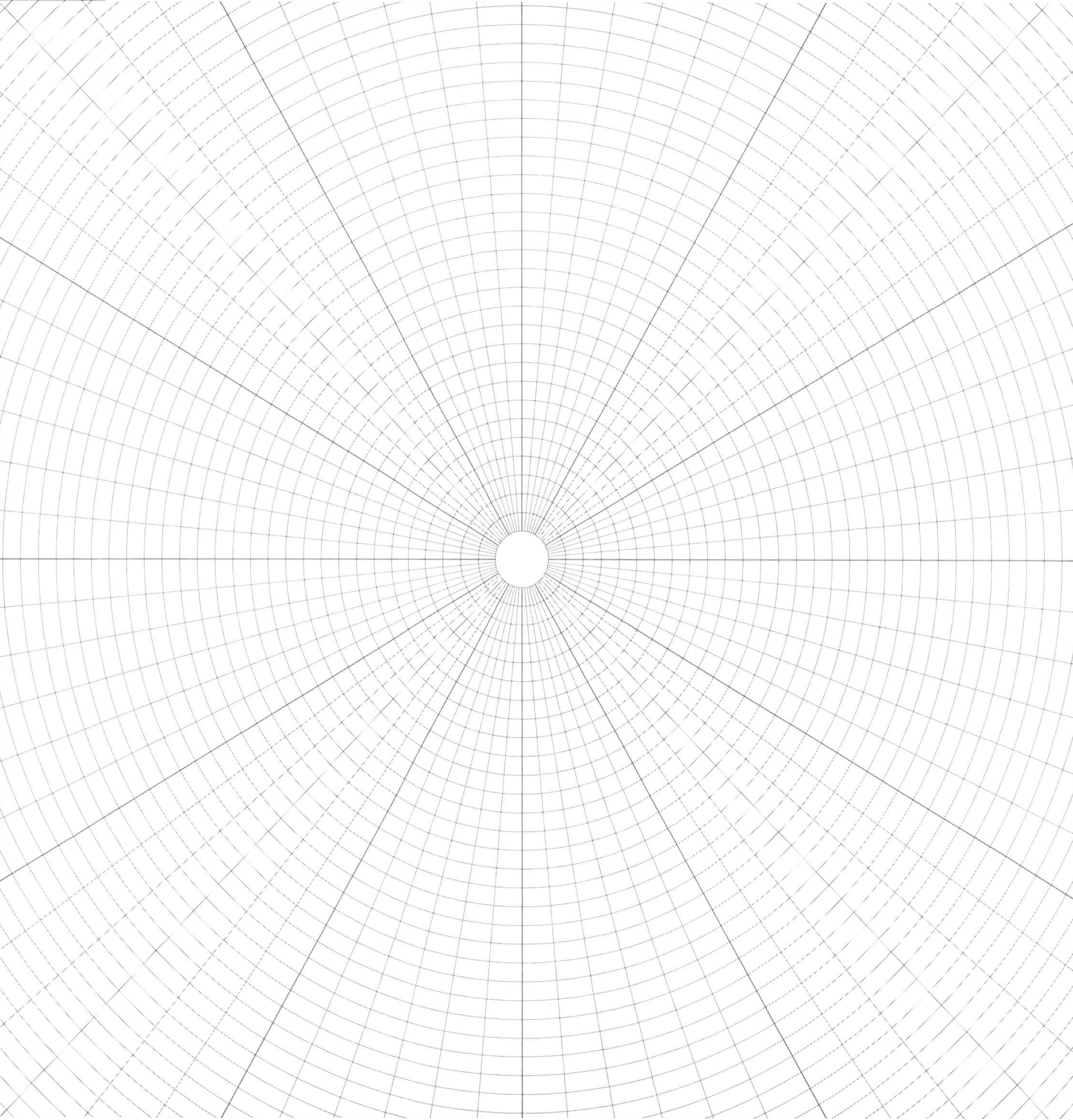

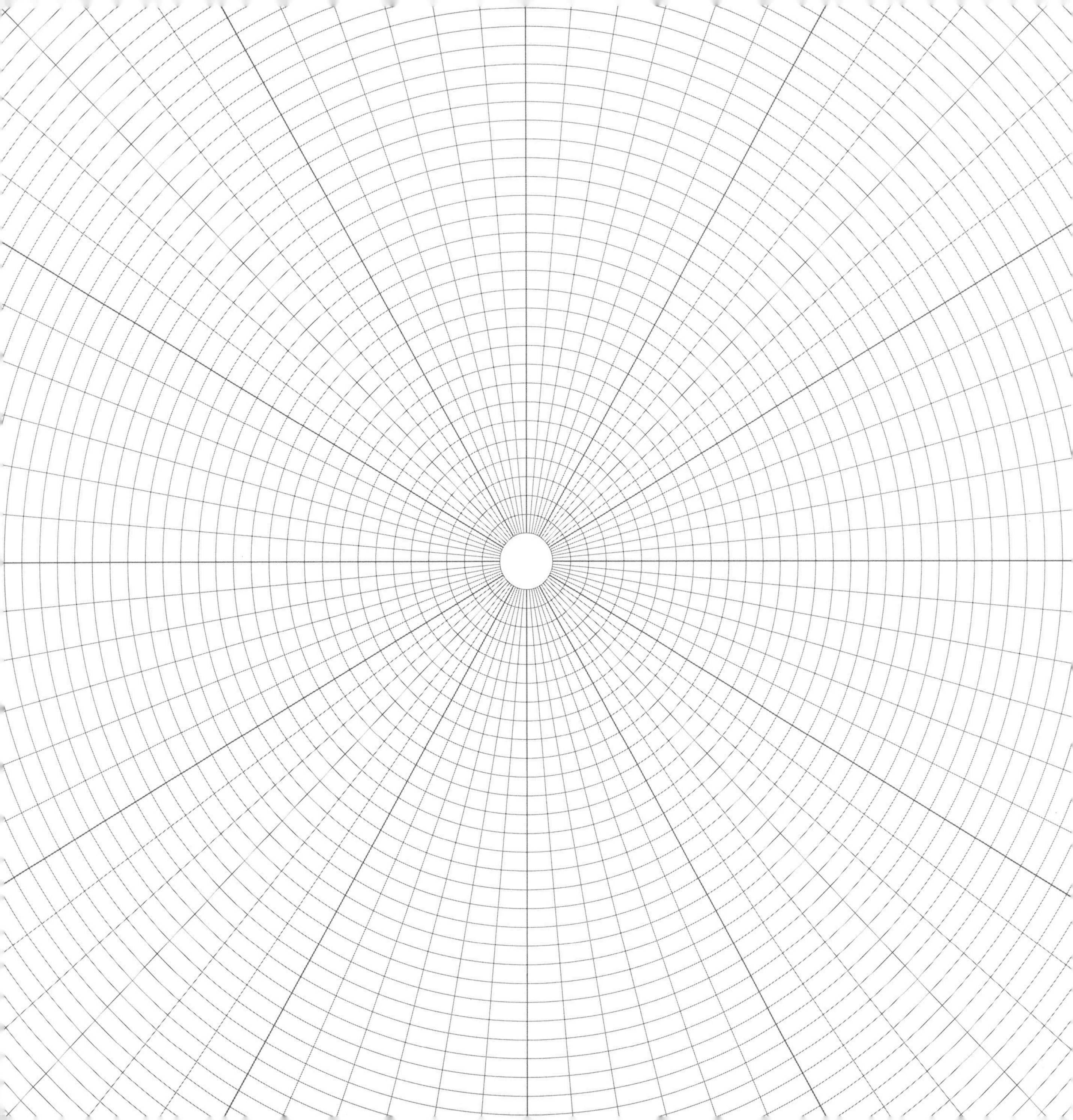

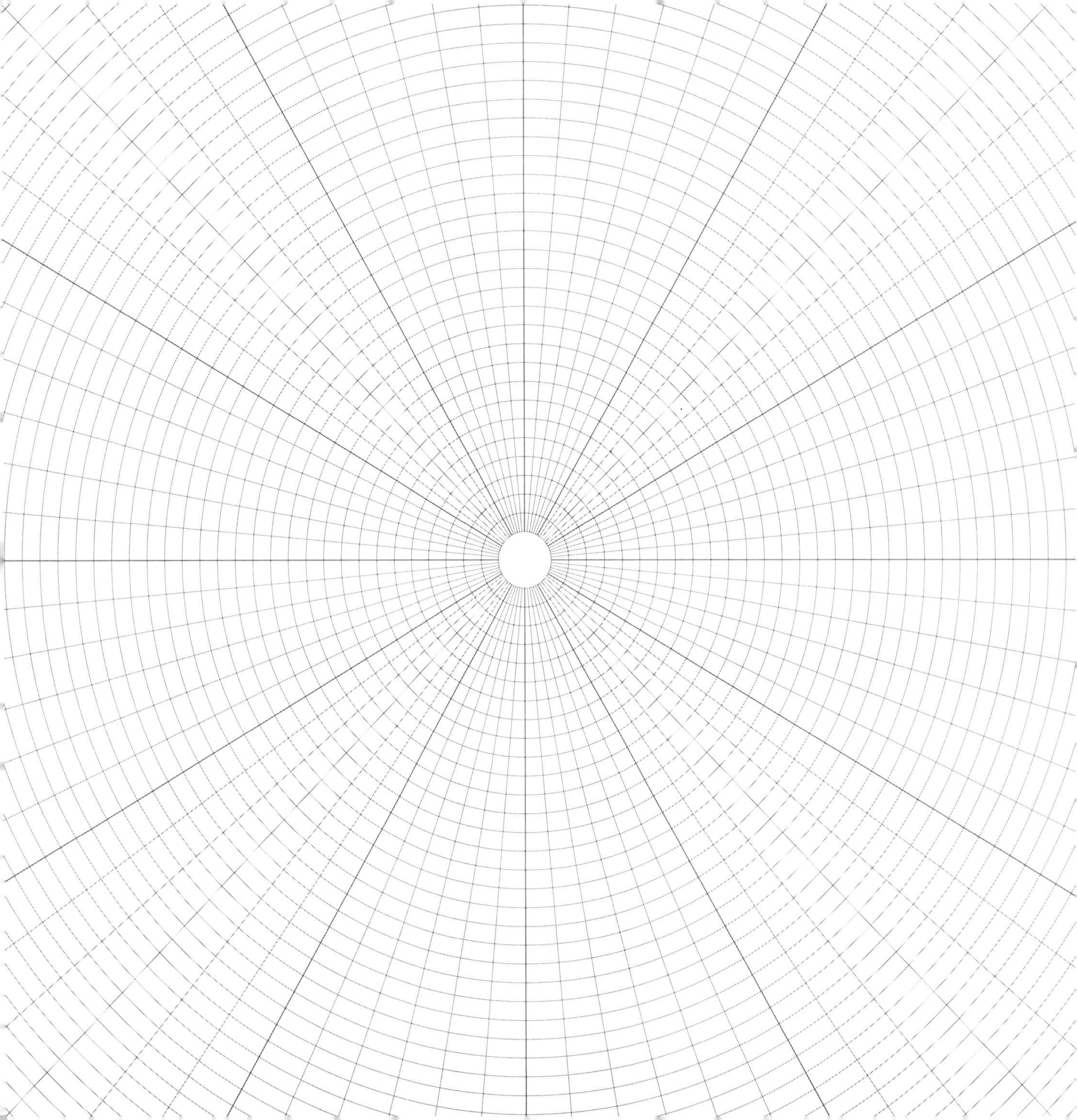